Classical

SUNDAY SCHOOL

Teacher's Manual

To learn more about Classical education,
and for great tips on teaching this course,
go to StrongHappyFamily.org.

There's a funny scene in chapter four of *Tom Sawyer*, where Tom is in Sunday School wishing to win the coveted prize: a Bible. To earn this award, the students are required to memorize verses; they collect tickets for each Scripture they recite, and save up those tickets in the hopes of one day receiving a Bible. Of course Tom doesn't have enough discipline (or tickets) to win honestly, but he wheels and deals and cheats his way to the prize. (When the visiting judge asks Tom to display some of his vast knowledge, Twain's genius for humor is instead displayed.)

How many tickets did Tom need to snag his Bible?

Two thousand!

When she was 12, Laura Ingalls Wilder, the author of the beloved *Little House* books, won a Bible for perfectly reciting 104 verses in one sitting.

One hundred four!

I tell these stories to demonstrate how differently children of a bygone generation learned the Bible. There was a time in our history when most Americans, regardless of their religious affiliations, knew the outline of the Bible, along with its "greatest hits." Average citizens understood literature that included biblical allusions, and could quote lyrical passages from the Shepherd's Psalm and the Sermon on the Mount. The Bible was once regarded as a cornerstone of Western Civilization, and no person considered himself educated if he hadn't digested its contents.

As post-modernism took over the academy, the Bible was tossed aside as an irrelevant relic of primitive societies. With the Book's expulsion, our culture didn't just lose a great work of literature; it also lost the fount of ethical teaching that had transformed the barbarian world.

Christians in America protested the Bible's expulsion from the classroom. They retained a reverence for the Scriptures, and understood the Bible's vital role in Western Civilization. Yet sadly, many churches adopted contemporary *approaches* to education. While rejecting the content of Post-Modern teaching, they adopted Post-modern teaching *methods* that featured flux, flow and fragmentation. Traditional content mastery, with its emphasis on Biblical literacy became a thing of the past. The result?

Many Christians became Biblically illiterate.

People who grew up in the church didn't choose to become biblically illiterate. They attended services and youth group events and Sunday school. They were often bright, attentive and serious about pursuing their faith.

Yet modern Christian education failed them. It presented a grab bag of disjointed Bible stories, occurring in a timeless netherworld, in a "far away land." Narnia and Nazareth blurred in their minds. No teacher expected them to retain or recite—because really, nothing of substance was usually taught. There was always a nice take-away moral like, "Be loving," or "Trust in God," however, the nature of this God, and the quality of His love were glossed over. The Christian faith was presented as kind-of, sort-of true—as long as you didn't inspect it too closely.

Biblical illiteracy has dire consequences

Predictably, many young people who craved solid food but were given only pabulum lost their appetite for serious Biblical study. Some concluded that there must not be much to Christianity, since none of their teachers could offer them anything that engaged their minds. They settled for a "little Christianity," with a tiny, manageable "god" who could be placed on a shelf next to their X-Box and taken down for weddings, funerals and job hunts.

The majority of young people who grew up in the church, however, have abandoned the faith entirely. Millennials, who crave authenticity, find very little of it in churches that claim to esteem the Bible above all things, but never bother to teach it seriously.

What do you imagine is in store for a society where even the children of the remnant reject Biblical truth? Read the newspaper.

The good news is that this trend can be reversed!

All is not lost. The Bible reminds us that there can be rebirth and renewal in society when people rediscover the Scriptures. King Josiah led a renaissance during a very bleak period in Judah's history when his priest Hilkiah uncovered the Book of the Law.

We can introduce the Scriptures to our children, and re-introduce the Scriptures to their parents. But we cannot use the pedagogy that created the problems in the first place. We need to look back to a method of teaching that entices the intellect, stokes curiosity, and lays a deep foundation. We need to rediscover the Classical Method.

The Classical Method described

The Classical Method divides a child's learning adventure into three stages: grammar, dialectic, and rhetoric, referred to collectively as the Trivium. During the grammar (or data) stage, a child's mind is like a thirsty sponge, absorbing information wherever it can. Kids in this stage memorize easily and are insatiably curious. In the dialectic state, a child begins to synthesize the data he's accumulated, connecting the dots and trying to understand how all of his stored information fits together. In the rhetoric stage, a young person begins to use his data-laden framework of the world to try to persuade and influence.

The three stages don't have sharp dividing lines, and there are elements of each of the stages that occur simultaneously throughout life. The Classical Method of education has been the gold standard for millennia, producing the great minds of the Western intellectual tradition. As modern educators have recoiled from the rigors of the Classical Method, modern students have suffered.

Clearly, this style of education is built on a foundation of *data*. Names, dates, locations, lists, descriptions. The more data a mind stores, the more dots it can connect, the more persuasive it can become. The broader the base, the taller the building.

This Sunday School Curriculum is designed using the Classical Method

The curriculum you hold in your hands is designed according to the Classical Method, for use in the *grammar stage*—typically with kids 4-11 or 12 years old. It contains data, and lots of it. There are maps, timelines, genealogies, memory passages, lists of kings and covenants and more.

But please remember: we present all this information not to puff up, or to show off. The vast amount of data is introduced so that when our students reach the rhetoric stage, their sweet minds will have information to massage and assemble. If a kid reaches the rhetoric stage, where his mind is longing to put pieces together to make sense of the world, and he finds that he's missing lots of pieces, he gets frustrated. And surly. And rude. We don't want frustrated, surly, rude teenagers, now do we?

Owning a broad base of data equips a child for the daunting task of making sense of the world, and eventually making his mark in it. Such knowledge also prevents a young person from falling prey to harmful fads and destructive ideologies. It's not so easy to dupe a kid who is armed with facts.

The design of this curriculum

The Classical Method employs cycled repetition. This means exposing a child to the same material several times, with ever deepening comprehension, throughout the course of his education.

Classical Sunday School is composed of twelve cycles, with twelve lessons in each cycle. The odd-numbered cycles each begin with Genesis and end in the Minor Prophets, highlighting different events in each cycle, spanning the entire Old Testament every twelve weeks. Similarly, the even-numbered cycles each begin in the Gospels and end near Revelation, highlighting different events each cycle, spanning the entire New Testament every twelve weeks. A church or home could easily master four cycles in a year, thus completing all the course material in three years. That means an individual child in this program would be taught all of this material at least twice in his childhood, and would have taken a tour of the whole Bible twelve times.

The skeleton of Classical Sunday School is a poem of the Bible's timeline set to the tune of "Mary Had a Little Lamb." We use familiar, catchy tunes to drill a lot of our data. This song takes you from Genesis to Revelation, listing the major events and personalities, and providing "hooks" on which new information may be hung. The timeline song is repeated weekly, while new data is introduced and placed on those hooks. The good news is that this same timeline song is repeated in every drill book: the first book might be challenging, but it will get easier as you progress through the cycles. The complete poem is found at the end of each drill book, and we learn it three entries at a time.

The components of the curriculum

The data introduced each week falls into the following categories:

Mapwork: Students will learn the major geographical features of the Ancient World, including rivers, mountains and deserts. Major cities and countries will be drilled as they pertain to that week's topic. Mapwork is important because it reminds a child that the events he studies in the Bible occurred in a real place on the globe, not in a mythical land.

Each lesson includes a blank outline map of the setting of the featured story, along with a list of places to identify. Ask your younger children to point on the map to where those places are; invite your older children to draw a map for themselves. Complete labeled maps are found at the end of each drill book.

Timeline: Students learn to recite and draw a timeline of the Bible, and insert people or episodes on the timeline. This reinforces the fact that the Bible discusses *historical* events.

In most of the lessons there is a rudimentary timeline sketched out. For Old Testament cycles (the odd-numbered ones) it looks like this:

_____A_____M_____D_____E_____
         2000   1500   1000   500

The letters "A, M, D and E," representing "Abraham, Moses, David and Exile," are spaced out at 500-year intervals. A mnemonic that always sticks with kids is that Sunday school is, "**A M**ost **D**elightful **E**xperience."

In the New Testament cycles (the even-numbered ones), the dates are somewhat evenly spaced, but not quite as memorable:

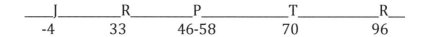

	J	R	P	T	R
	-4	33	46-58	70	96

The letters on the line represent, " Jesus' birth, Resurrection, Paul's Journeys, Temple Destruction, Revelation Vision." A mnemonic to remember the New Testament milestone is this little poem, set to the refrain of "Jingle Bells":

> **J**esus' birth, His **R**esurrection
> **P**aul's trips, **T**emple destruction,
> **R**evelation to St. John,
> The New Testament is done.

Each day when you drill, ask your child to point on the timeline to when this week's Bible lesson (found dead-center on the page under the cycle number) occurred. Older children might be asked to draw the timeline themselves, marking the featured event.

Hymns: Because many churches prefer to perform modern worship songs in services, most young people are unfamiliar with traditional hymns. This is a shame because many of the old hymns winsomely teach Bible and theology. We focus on learning one hymn every four weeks or so. We add a new verse each week, always reviewing what was previously taught.

We have nothing against modern worship songs and choruses; many of them are quite lovely. But our Christian musical heritage is quite rich and vast, and we want to expose children to our sacred hymnary. The lyrics of these traditional songs have encouraged, instructed and comforted believers throughout the centuries, and their poetry has given voice to the praise of martyrs.

Ancient Languages: Hebrew and Greek are the original languages of the Bible, and any advanced study of the Scriptures would require fluency in those languages. With our introduction, a motivated junior high student could jump right in to the study of Biblical languages.

Learning Biblical languages might seem scarier to you than to your kids. Play it cool. Most kids love learning how to draw letters in Hebrew and Greek—and you might too! Just pick up a crayon, draw the letter and say its name. Easy!

We slowly introduce the alphabets and some basic words in the Biblical languages—Hebrew in the odd-numbered Old Testament cycles, and Greek in the even-numbered New Testament cycles.

Passage Memory: The discipline of memorizing the Scriptures returns tremendous dividends. God's Word hidden in a child's heart will comfort, correct, warn and encourage him throughout his life. Particularly useful is the habit of memorizing whole passages of Scriptures, where God's Words cannot be wrenched from their context or misapplied. Further, a child memorizing whole passages becomes aware of the lyrical beauty of the Scriptures, and begins to fall in love with those words.

Bible Fact Song: It is really helpful in understanding the broad sweep of the Scriptures to have certain facts memorized: the kings of Judah, the Levitical Feasts, the Disciples, the covenants, etc. We teach these and many other "lists" by putting the words to the tune of a familiar children's song.

In the classroom

A Classical Sunday School teacher will introduce all of the week's new grammar in a single class. This will include the Bible timeline song, mapwork, a timeline, a hymn, some Hebrew (in the odd-numbered cycles) or Greek (in the even-numbered cycles), part of a memory passage, and a Bible fact song.

Additionally, the teacher will recount a story from the Bible. The teacher might read the story directly from the Scriptures, or may tell the story in his own words, or use an excellent resource that is true to the text. The teacher's creativity and love of the Scriptures will be on display here. This curriculum does not give the teacher a "script" to follow in teaching this lesson, but simply assigns the topic. [A teacher who cannot present a Bible story without a script should probably not be teaching this (or any?) Sunday school class.]

Parents are encouraged to be a part of the class! This aids the teacher in keeping the class focused, and also gives parents a preview of the work to be reviewed during the week. And any parent who might have suffered from a post-modern style of content-free education can learn this information right alongside his child. It's never too late to learn!

This curriculum is designed to be drilled at home.

In the Classical Method, students are expected to memorize the data presented in the grammar stage. While glancing at the information won't harm a child, he won't fully benefit from the exposure unless his "owns" the data. When a mind can quickly retrieve facts, it can more deftly assemble arguments. But memorization won't occur unless drilling takes place at home.

Drilling the week's material should take only 10-15 minutes a day, and it's best to do it at the same time each day—during breakfast or right before bed perhaps. You'll be amazed by how much your kids (and you!) will retain with simple daily drilling.

There are small, colorful drill books to accompany each 12-week cycle of the curriculum. Since all the grades of a Sunday school are covering the same material, only one drill book is needed per family for each cycle.

There are parents who might think, "I just don't have time to teach the Bible to my children everyday." My reply is, "You have time for whatever you think is important." If you agree that instructing your children in the bedrock of Western Civilization and the ultimate standard of ethical behavior is important, then you'll find the time to drill. If I check Facebook everyday because it's important to me, I better find time to teach my kids the Bible.

Some tips for memorizing

I have an actor friend who often performs Shakespeare, and is required to memorize long scripts. He told me that the key to memorizing anything is to **say it eleven times in a row**. From my experience, this almost always works! Kids are often delighted to repeat words if there is variety: "Say this after me in a monster voice." "Repeat this talking like a cowboy." "Can you recite this while standing on one foot?" "I bet the girls in this room can say this louder than the boys can!"

With a little creativity, a roomful of children will laugh their way through memorizing data. Keep it light, don't mind a little noise, and laugh along with your students.

Material required

This curriculum guide and a Bible are the only books a teacher will need to teach this three-year course. When the course cycles are completed, it's time to begin again. Consider the efficiency: once a church purchases a curriculum guide for each classroom, it will never need to invest in any more teaching materials. Ever. No monthly packets to distribute, no recurring billing, no forests-full of consumables to process.

For the course to be really effective, each family enrolled in the class should have an inexpensive drill book for use at home each cycle. These drill books are priced very modestly to ensure that churches will provide one for each family involved. They can be reused every three years.

Kids will need paper and pencils or crayons for drawing maps, timelines and Hebrew and Greek letters, and the teacher should have a white board and markers.

When your church enrolls and purchases the *Curriculum Guide*, you'll be eligible to download songs and other helpful resources from our website.

Though they are not required texts for this course, we recommend two excellent classics for teaching Bible stories at church and at home, both available at our website:

> *Hurlbut's Story of the Bible* was the best-selling Sunday school resource at the beginning of the 20th century. It narrates the Bible in 168 stories, suitable for children between the ages of 6 and 12. The author describes geographical features and historical background when they are useful.
>
> Catherine F. Vos's *The Child's Story Bible*, published in 1935, is a sweet, gentle retelling of the Bible in 202 lessons. Children from 3-10 years of age would benefit from Mrs. Vos's faithful rendering of the Bible's stories.

Both authors convey an enthusiasm for the Scriptures that is contagious. They wrote at a time when adults believed that children really could comprehend great ideas if they were explained well. Reading just one chapter a day of either of these books will provide a child with the entire narrative of redemption from Genesis to Revelation in less than a year. The Curriculum Guide denotes which chapters of Hurlbut's and Vos correspond to the lesson taught in Sunday school that week.

Kids can and will learn a lot if they think we expect them to!

When Jesus was a boy, Bar Mitzvah candidates were expected to have memorized the Pentateuch: Genesis, Exodus, Leviticus, Numbers and Deuteronomy. Americans at 4th of July gatherings in the 19th century all recited the Declaration of Independence together—the whole thing, not just the Preamble. Eighteen-year-olds studying for the clergy at Yale during the colonial era were not taught Greek or Hebrew, because they were expected to be fully literate in those ancient languages before matriculation.

Young people can and will learn a great deal if they think we expect it of them. Without effort, kids will memorize the jingles and pop songs they hear. Just imagine if we expose our kids to a wealth of Biblical knowledge!

When I was a youth group leader years ago, the young, energetic youth pastor could not get his group of 60 junior high students to settle down and pay attention to his lesson. It frustrated him terribly. I mentioned to him that perhaps his lessons were too easy, and that the kids were bored. I suggested that he teach a really challenging study, hard enough that kids would have to scramble to keep up. He told me I was crazy—that if the kids couldn't understand his simple lesson, how would they understand a difficult one? But he took my suggestion anyway.

The kids responded with focused attention! They felt respected by their teacher, and they returned the respect. Best of all, the kids began eagerly studying the Scriptures and applying those teachings to their lives. They discovered for themselves that the Bible really *is* an interesting book, and that it holds all kinds of useful information.

This curriculum respects a child's intellect, and conveys that we expect great things from our students. Children will eagerly respond to this message.

Hold the crown high, and let the child grow into it.

The end result

Always remember, the goal of all this knowledge is not vanity; we endeavor to fill our children's minds with valuable information so that they can process and assemble that information as teenagers, and then become useful servants of the King as adults.

In the parable of the talents, the servant who neglected his master's gift was sharply rebuked, while the servants who received the master's gifts and put them to work were greeted with the commendation, "Well done, good and faithful servant."

Our minds are among God's greatest gifts to us. Luke 10:27 commands us, "Love the Lord your God with all your heart and with all your soul and with all your strength and with all your *mind*." This curriculum will help you to obey that command, so that you might one day hear from our Master, "Well done, good and faithful servant."

TWELVE CYCLE OVERVIEW

BIBLE FACTS	BIBLE MEMORY	HYMNS	ANCIENT LANG.	MAPS	TIME-LINE
Days of Creation Abraham's Descendants 1 Jacob's Descendants	Psalm 1	Amazing Grace The Church's One Foundation Holy, Holy, Holy	Hebrew Alphabet	Middle East	Genesis to Malachi
Names of Jesus Twelve Disciples 2 Apostles' Creed	1 Corinthians 13	It Is Well Come, Thou Almighty King Praise to the Lord, the Almighty	Greek Alphabet	Mediter-ranean	John the Baptist to Revelation
Old Testament Books The 10 Commandments 3 The Judges	Isaiah 53	Be Thou My Vision All Creatures of Our God and King All Hail the Power of Jesus' Name	Hebrew Alphabet	Middle East	Genesis to Malachi
New Testament Books The Fruit of the Spirit 4 Prophecies about Jesus	Colossians 1:15-23	Blessed Assurance When I Survey the Wondrous Cross O Worship the King	Greek Alphabet	Mediter-ranean	John the Baptist to Revelation
Plagues in Egypt The Feasts of the Lord 5 Covenants	Exodus 20:2-17	Jesus Paid it All A Mighty Fortress Is Our God Crown Him with Many Crowns	The Shema	Middle East	Genesis to Malachi
Paul's Journeys Sayings on the Cross 6 Review	Philippians 2:1-11	Come Thou Fount of Every Blessing How Firm a Foundation Come, Ye Thankful People	1 John 4:16 John 1:1	Mediter-ranean	John the Baptist to Revelation
The Tabernacle Names of God 7 Old Testament Offerings	Deuteronomy 6:4-9 Psalm 23	What a Friend We Have in Jesus O Worship the King America the Beautiful	Hebrew Alphabet	Middle East	Genesis to Malachi
Miracles of Jesus Attributes of God 8 Churches in Revelation	John 1:1-14	The Old Rugged Cross And Can it Be? Be Still My Soul	Greek Alphabet	Mediter-ranean	John the Baptist to Revelation
9 The Kings of Judah	Genesis 1:1-2, 1:26-2:3	He Leadeth Me Standing on the Promises of God Just as I Am	Hebrew Alphabet	Middle East	Genesis to Malachi
10 Cathechism	Matthew 5:3-20	Now Thank We All Our God Take My Life and Let it Be I Know Whom I Have Believed	Greek Alphabet	Mediter-ranean	John the Baptist to Revelation
Hebrew Calendar Daniel's Statue 11 Review	Proverbs 3:1-12	Joyful, Joyful, We Adore Thee Rock of Ages Battle Hymn of the Republic	The Shema	Middle East	Genesis to Malachi
The Lord's Prayer Armor of God 12 Review	1 Corinthians 15:50-58 John 14:1-3	Alas and Did My Savior Bleed? Christ the Lord Is Risen Today Faith of our Fathers	1 John 4:16 John 1:1	Mediter-ranean	John the Baptist to Revelation

Classical
Sunday School

FAMILY DRILL BOOK

CYCLES 1 & 2

To learn more about Classical education, and for
great tips on using this Drill Book, go to
StrongHappyFamily.org

BIBLE FACTS

Days of Creation

DAY 1: Day and night

DAY 2: Sky and water

DAY 3: Land and plants

DAY 4: Sun, moon and stars

DAY 5: Birds and fish

DAY 6: Animals and man

DAY 7: God rested

TIMELINE

Creation

Fall

Cain and Abel

hymn

AMAZING GRACE
verse 1

Amazing grace,
how sweet the sound,
That saved a wretch
like me.
I once was lost,
but now I'm found.
'Twas blind,
but now I see.

I PRACTICED:

☆ ☆ ☆ ☆ ☆ ☆

M	T	W	T	F	S
O	U	E	H	R	A
N	E	D	U	I	T

CYCLE 1

CREATION

WEEK 1

PSALM 1:1a

Blessed is
the man
who does not walk
in the counsel
of the wicked

related stories

Genesis 1-2

Vos Old
Testament
Lessons 1-4

Hurlbut Part 1
Lesson 1

Aleph
א

Bet
ב

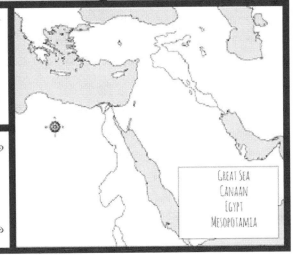

Great Sea
Canaan
Egypt
Mesopotamia

BIBLE FACTS

DAYS OF CREATION

DAY 1: Day and night

DAY 2: Sky and water

DAY 3: Land and plants

DAY 4: Sun, moon and stars

DAY 5: Birds and fish

DAY 6: Animals and man

DAY 7: God rested

TIMELINE

Flood

Job

Tower of Babel

hymn

AMAZING GRACE
verse 2

'Twas Grace that taught,
my heart to fear.
And grace,
my fears relieved.
How precious did
that grace appear,
The hour I first believed.

I PRACTICED:

☆ ☆ ☆ ☆ ☆ ☆

M	T	W	T	F	S
O	U	E	H	R	A
N	E	D	U	I	T

CYCLE 1
FLOOD
WEEK 2

PSALM 1:1b

or stand in the
way of sinners
or sit in
the seat
of mockers.

related stories

Genesis 6-9

Vos Old
Testament
Lesson 10

Hurlbut Part 1
Lessons 3-4

Gimel
ג

Dalet
ד

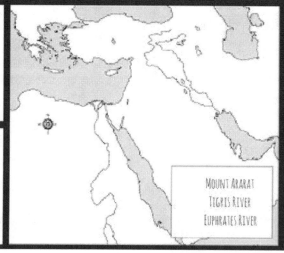

MOUNT ARARAT
TIGRIS RIVER
EUPHRATES RIVER

BIBLE FACTS

Days of Creation

DAY 1: Day and night

DAY 2: Sky and water

DAY 3: Land and plants

DAY 4: Sun, moon and stars

DAY 5: Birds and fish

DAY 6: Animals and man

DAY 7: God rested

TIMELINE

Abraham

Ishmael

Sodom and Gomorrah

A	M	D	E
2000	1500	1000	500

hymn

AMAZING GRACE
verse 3

Through many dangers,
toils and snares,
I have already come;
'Tis grace hath brought
me safe thus far,
And grace will lead
me home.

I PRACTICED:

☆ ☆ ☆ ☆ ☆ ☆
M T W T F S
O U E H R A
N E D U I T

CYCLE 1

ABRAHAM

WEEK 3

PSALM 1:2a

But his delight
is in the law
of the Lord,

related stories

Genesis 12-25

Vos Old
Testament
Lesson 12

Hurlbut Part 1
Lesson 5

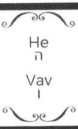
He
ה

Vav
ו

UR
CHALDEA
HARAN
CANAAN

BIBLE FACTS

Days of Creation

DAY 1: Day and night

DAY 2: Sky and water

DAY 3: Land and plants

DAY 4: Sun, moon and stars

DAY 5: Birds and fish

DAY 6: Animals and man

DAY 7: God rested

TIMELINE

Isaac as well

Jacob and Esau

Israel's tribes

_A_	_M_	_D_	_E_
2000	1500	1000	500

hymn

AMAZING GRACE
verse 4

The Lord has promised
good to me,
His Word
my hope secures;
He will my Shield
and Portion be,
As long as life endures.

I PRACTICED:

☆ ☆ ☆ ☆ ☆ ☆

M	T	W	T	F	S
O	U	E	H	R	A
N	E	D	U	I	T

CYCLE 1
ISAAC
WEEK 4

PSALM 1:2b

and on his law
he meditates
day and night.

related stories

Genesis 21-29

Vos Old Testament Lessons 16-17

Hurlbut Part 1 Lessons 10-11

Zayin
ז

Het
ח

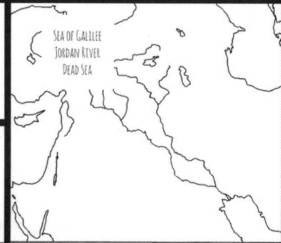

SEA OF GALILEE
JORDAN RIVER
DEAD SEA

BIBLE FACTS

ABRAHAM'S DESCENDANTS
To the tune of "London Bridges"

Abraham and Sarah, Sarah, Sarah,
Abraham and Sarah had baby Isaac.

Isaac and Rebekah, Rebekah, Rebekah,
Isaac and Rebekah had Jacob and Esau.

Jacob and Rachel, and Leah, and
Bilhah, and the last one, Zilpah,
Had the sons of Israel.

TIMELINE

Joseph in Egypt

Moses' Life

Burning bush and plagues in Egypt

_A_	M	D	E_
2000	1500	1000	500

hymn

THE CHURCH HAS ONE FOUNDATION
verse 1

The church has one foundation,
'Tis Jesus Christ her Lord;
She is His new creation,
Through water by the word.
From heav'n He came and sought her
To be His holy bride;
With His own blood He bought her,
And for her life He died.

I PRACTICED:

☆ ☆ ☆ ☆ ☆ ☆

M	T	W	T	F	S
O	U	E	H	R	A
N	E	D	U	I	T

CYCLE 1

JOSEPH

WEEK 5

PSALM 1:3a

He is like a tree
planted by streams
of water,
which yields
its fruit in season

related stories

Genesis 37-50

Vos Old Testament Lessons 24-31

Hurlbut Part 1 Lessons 15-19

Tet
ט

Yod
י

MIDIAN
GOSHEN
NILE RIVER
EGYPT

BIBLE FACTS

Abraham's Descendants

To the tune of "London Bridges"

Abraham and Sarah, Sarah, Sarah,
Abraham and Sarah had baby Isaac.

Isaac and Rebekah, Rebekah, Rebekah,
Isaac and Rebekah had Jacob and Esau.

Jacob and Rachel, and Leah, and
Bilhah, and the last one, Zilpah,
Had the sons of Israel.

TIMELINE

Exodus and 10 Commandments

Desert, Ark, Feasts, Tabernacle

Joshua's Conquest

A	M	D	E
2000	1500	1000	500

hymn

THE CHURCH HAS ONE FOUNDATION
verse 2

Elect from every nation,
Yet one o'er all the earth,
Her charter of salvation—
One Lord, one faith, one birth.
One holy name she blesses,
Partakes one holy food;
And to one hope she presses,
With every grace endued.

I PRACTICED:

☆ ☆ ☆ ☆ ☆ ☆

M	T	W	T	F	S
O	U	E	H	R	A
N	E	D	U	I	T

CYCLE 1
Exodus and Law
WEEK 6

PSALM 1:3b

and whose leaf
does not wither.
Whatever he
does prospers.

related stories

Exodus 12-20

Vos Old Testament
Lessons 35-39

Hurlbut Part 1
Lessons 24-26

Kaf
כ
ך

Lamed
ל

Red Sea
Mount Sinai
Sinai Desert

BIBLE FACTS

Abraham's Descendants
To the tune of "London Bridges"

Abraham and Sarah, Sarah, Sarah,
Abraham and Sarah had baby Isaac.

Isaac and Rebekah, Rebekah, Rebekah,
Isaac and Rebekah had Jacob and Esau.

Jacob and Rachel, and Leah, and
Bilhah, and the last one, Zilpah,
Had the sons of Israel.

TIMELINE

Judges rule

Ruth and Boaz

King Saul's reign

A	M	D	E
2000	1500	1000	500

hymn

THE CHURCH HAS ONE FOUNDATION
verse 3

Long with a scornful wonder
Men saw her sore oppressed,
By schisms rent asunder,
By heresies distressed.
Yet saints their watch were keeping
To hail a brighter day,
When God should stop their weeping.
Take their reproach away.

I PRACTICED:

☆ ☆ ☆ ☆ ☆ ☆

M	T	W	T	F	S
O	U	E	H	R	A
N	E	D	U	I	T

CYCLE 1

Judges rule
WEEK 7

Psalm 1:4

Not so
the wicked!
They are
like chaff
that the wind
blows away.

related stories

Judges 1-21

Vos Old
Testament
Lessons 57-63

Hurlbut Part 2
Lessons 6-17

Mem
נ
ם

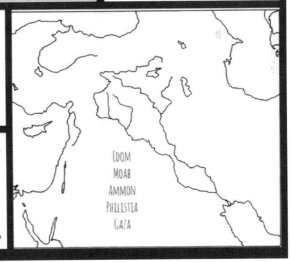

EDOM
MOAB
AMMON
PHILISTIA
GAZA

BIBLE FACTS

ABRAHAM'S DESCENDANTS

TO THE TUNE OF "LONDON BRIDGES"

Abraham and Sarah, Sarah, Sarah,
Abraham and Sarah had baby Isaac.

Isaac and Rebekah, Rebekah, Rebekah,
Isaac and Rebekah had Jacob and Esau.

Jacob and Rachel, and Leah, and
Bilhah, and the last one, Zilpah,
Had the sons of Israel.

TIMELINE

David's Kingdom

Psalms, Covenant

Solomon's Temple,
Kingdom divides

A	M	D	E
2000	1500	1000	500

hymn

THE CHURCH HAS ONE
FOUNDATION
verse 5

Back to the one foundation,
From sects and creeds made free,
Come saints of every nation
To blessed unity.
Once more the ancient glory
Shines as in days of old,
And tells the wondrous story:
One God, one faith, one fold.

I PRACTICED:

☆ ☆ ☆ ☆ ☆ ☆

M	T	W	T	F	S
O	U	E	H	R	A
N	E	D	U	I	T

CYCLE 1
David's Kingdom
WEEK 8

Psalm 1:5a

Therefore
the wicked
will not stand
in the judgment,

related stories

2 Samuel 1-24
1 Kings 1-2

Vos Old
Testament
Lessons 72-75

Hurlbut Part 3
Lessons 10-16

Nun

ﬨ
ﬧ

Jerusalem
Bethlehem
Philistia
Gath
Tyre and Sidon

BIBLE FACTS

Jacob's Descendants

To the tune of "Jacob's Ladder"

Reuben, Simeon, Levi, Judah,

Issachar, Zebulun, Joseph,

Benjamin,

Naphtali, Dan, Gad and Asher,

Sons of Israel

TIMELINE

Ahab and Elijah on the north side

Hezekiah and Isaiah in the South

Israel falls to Assyria's clout

A	M	D	E
2000	1500	1000	500

hymn

HOLY, HOLY, HOLY
verse 1

Holy, holy, holy!
Lord God Almighty!
Early in the morning
our song shall rise to Thee;
Holy, holy, holy,
merciful and mighty!
God in three Persons,
blessed Trinity!

I PRACTICED:

☆ ☆ ☆ ☆ ☆ ☆

M	T	W	T	F	S
O	U	E	H	R	A
N	E	D	U	I	T

CYCLE 1
Ahab and Elijah
WEEK 9

Psalm 1:5b

nor sinners
in the assembly
of the righteous.

related stories

1 Kings 17-22
2 Kings 1-2

Vos Old Testament
Lessons 80-89

Hurlbut Part 4
Lessons 2-16

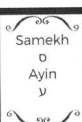
Samekh
ס
Ayin
ע

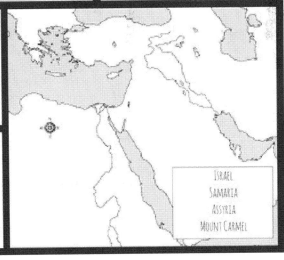
Israel
Samaria
Assyria
Mount Carmel

BIBLE FACTS

Jacob's Descendants
To the tune of "Jacob's Ladder"

Reuben, Simeon, Levi, Judah,

Issachar, Zebulun, Joseph,

Benjamin,

Naphtali, Dan, Gad and Asher,

Sons of Israel

TIMELINE

Jeremiah and Ezekiel
warn Judah

Judah falls to Babylon,
Temple ruined

Daniel in the Exile

A	M	D	E
2000	1500	1000	500

hymn

HOLY, HOLY, HOLY
verse 2

Holy, holy, holy!
All the saints adore Thee,
Casting down their
golden crowns
around the glassy sea;
Cherubim and seraphim
falling down before Thee,
Which wert and art and
evermore shall be.

I PRACTICED:
☆ ☆ ☆ ☆ ☆ ☆
M T W T F S
O U E H R A
N E D U I T

CYCLE 1
Jeremiah and Ezekiel
WEEK 10

Psalm 1:6a

For the Lord
watches over
the way of the
righteous,

related stories
Jeremiah 1-52
Ezekiel 1-48

Vos Old
Testament
Lessons 98-99

Hurlbut Part 5
Lessons 1-18

Pe
פ
ף
Tsadi
צ
ץ

JUDAH
BABYLON
MOUNT ZION

BIBLE FACTS

Jacob's Descendants

To the tune of "Jacob's Ladder"

Reuben, Simeon, Levi, Judah,

Issachar, Zebulun, Joseph,

Benjamin,

Naphtali, Dan, Gad and Asher,

Sons of Israel

CYCLE 1
Cyrus' Decree
WEEK 11

TIMELINE

Cyrus' decree
Exiles return

Temple rebuilding

Esther saves the
Jews

_A_	_M_	_D_	_E_
2000	1500	1000	500

hymn

HOLY, HOLY, HOLY
verse 3

Holy, holy, holy!
Though the darkness hide
Thee,
Though the eye of sinful man
Thy glory may not see;
Only Thou art holy;
there is none beside Thee,
Perfect in pow'r, in love, and
purity.

Psalm 1:6b

but the way
of the wicked
will perish.

related stories

Ezra 5

Vos Old
Testament
Lessons 105-106

Hurlbut Part 5
Lesson 13

Qof
ק

Resh
ר

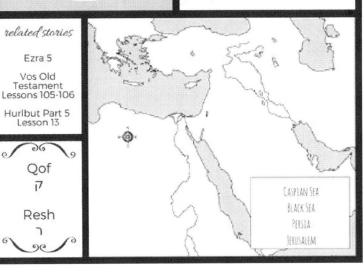

CASPIAN SEA
BLACK SEA
PERSIA
JERUSALEM

BIBLE FACTS

Jacob's Descendants
To the tune of "Jacob's Ladder"

Reuben, Simeon, Levi, Judah,

Issachar, Zebulun, Joseph,

Benjamin,

Naphtali, Dan, Gad and Asher,

Sons of Israel

Nehemiah builds the wall

Malachi foretells John the Baptist's call

Maccabean period ends here, no word from God for 400 years

_A_____M_____D____E__
2000   1500   1000   500

hymn

HOLY, HOLY, HOLY
verse 4

Holy, holy, holy!
Lord God Almighty!
All Thy works shall praise Thy Name,
in earth, and sky, and sea;
Holy, holy, holy;
merciful and mighty!
God in three Persons,
blessed Trinity!

I PRACTICED:
☆ ☆ ☆ ☆ ☆ ☆
M T W T F S
O U E H R A
N E D U I T

CYCLE 1
Nehemiah builds the wall
WEEK 12

Psalm 1

REVIEW!

related stories

Nehemiah 1-13

Vos Old Testament Lesson 110

Hurlbut Part 5 Lesson 17

Shin
ש

Tav
ת

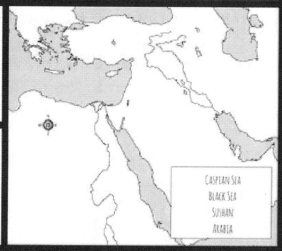

Caspian Sea
Black Sea
Sushan
Arabia

BIBLE FACTS

Jesus' Names, Verse 1

To the tune of "You Are My Sunshine"

Alpha, Omega, Lion of Judah,

Messiah, Shepherd of the Sheep,

Immanuel, Friend, Lord of Glory,

Our Passover,

Our Great High Priest.

TIMELINE

John the Baptist

Messiah is born

Shepherds and
Magi visit the Lord

J	R	P	T	R
-5	33	46-58	70	96

hymn

IT IS WELL
verse 1

When peace, like a river,
attendeth my way,
When sorrows like sea billows
roll;
Whatever my lot,
Thou hast taught me to say,
It is well, it is well with my soul.

Refrain:
It is well with my soul,
It is well, it is well with my soul.

I PRACTICED:

☆ ☆ ☆ ☆ ☆

M	T	W	T	F	S
O	U	E	H	R	A
N	E	D	U	I	T

CYCLE 2

John the Baptist

WEEK 1

1 Corinthians 13:1

If I speak in the
tongues of men or
of angels,
but have not love,
I am only a
resounding gong or
a clanging cymbal.

related stories

Luke 1

Vos New
Testament
Lessons 1 & 25

Hurlbut Part 6
Lessons 1, 5, 18

Alpha
A α

Beta
B β

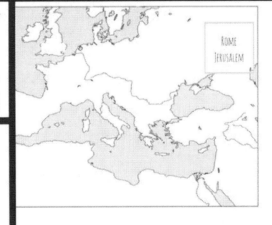

ROME

JERUSALEM

BIBLE FACTS

Jesus' Names, verse 2

To the tune of "You Are My Sunshine"

Prophet, Lord, Savior,

And King of all Kings,

Mediator 'tween God and Men,

Rock, Vine, Bread of Life,

And the Good Shepherd,

The Firstborn from the Dead.

TIMELINE

Flight into Egypt
Herod's Slaughter

Boy Jesus at the Temple

Baptism at the Jordan

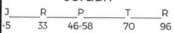

J	R	P	T	R
-5	33	46-58	70	96

hymn

IT IS WELL
verse 2

Though Satan should buffet,
though trials should come,
Let this blest assurance control,
That Christ hath regarded my
helpless estate,
And hath shed His own blood
for my soul.

Refrain:
It is well with my soul,
It is well, it is well with my soul.

I PRACTICED:

☆ ☆ ☆ ☆ ☆ ☆

M	T	W	T	F	S
O	U	E	H	R	A
N	E	D	U	I	T

CYCLE 2

Flight into Egypt

WEEK 2

1 Corinthians 13:2

If I have the gift of
prophecy and can
fathom all mysteries
and all knowledge,
and if I have a faith
that can move
mountains, but
have not love, I am
nothing.

related stories

Matthew 2

Vos New
Testament
Lessons 4-5

Hurlbut Part 6
Lesson 3

Gamma
Γ γ

Delta
Δ δ

Nazareth
Bethlehem
Egypt

BIBLE FACTS

Jesus' Names, verse 3

To the tune of "You Are My Sunshine"

Only Begotten of the Father,

Rabbi, the Seed of Abraham,

The Last Adam,

The Word Become Flesh,

Son of God, the Son of Man

TIMELINE

Temptation in the desert

Disciples' Call

Cana Wedding
Jubilee Inaugural

J	R	P		T	R
-5	33	46-58		70	96

hymn

IT IS WELL
verse 3

My sin—oh, the bliss of this
glorious thought!—
My sin, not in part
but the whole,
Is nailed to the cross,
and I bear it no more,
Praise the Lord, praise the Lord,
O my soul!

Refrain:
It is well with my soul,
It is well, it is well with my soul.

I PRACTICED:

☆ ☆ ☆ ☆ ☆ ☆

M	T	W	T	F	S
O	U	E	H	R	A
N	E	D	U	I	T

CYCLE 2
Temptation in the Desert
WEEK 3

1 Corinthians 13:3

If I give all I possess
to the poor
and surrender my
body to the flames,
but have not love,
I gain nothing.

related stories

Matthew 4
Luke 4

Vos New
Testament
Lesson 8

Hurlbut Part 6
Lesson 6

Epsilon
E ε

Zeta
Z ζ

Egypt
Jerusalem
Mount Tabor
Mount Hermon
Mount Zion

BIBLE FACTS

Jesus' Names, verse 4

To the tune of "You Are My Sunshine"

The Lord of all Lords,

God's Pascal Lamb,

Morning Star and Chief Cornerstone,

Light of the World,

Bread Come Down from Heaven,

Redeemer, Master, God's Holy One

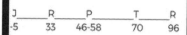

Jesus clears the
Temple, Ministry
begins

Meets Nicodemus and
the Samaritan

Sermon on the Mount

J	R	P	T	R
-5	33	46-58	70	96

hymn

IT IS WELL
verse 6

And Lord, haste the day
when the faith shall be sight,
The clouds be rolled back
as a scroll;
The trump shall resound,
and the Lord shall descend,
Even so, it is well with my soul.

Refrain:
It is well with my soul,
It is well, it is well with my soul.

I PRACTICED:

☆ ☆ ☆ ☆ ☆ ☆

M	T	W	T	F	S
O	U	E	H	R	A
N	E	D	U	I	T

CYCLE 2
Jesus' ministry begins
WEEK 4

1 Corinthians 13:4

Love is patient,
love is kind.
It does not envy,
it does not boast,
it is not proud.

related stories
John 2

Vos New
Testament
Lessons 11, 18, 34-
36, 40, 42

Hurlbut Part 6
Lessons 7, 10-12,
21-23, 29, 31

Eta
H η

Theta
Θ θ

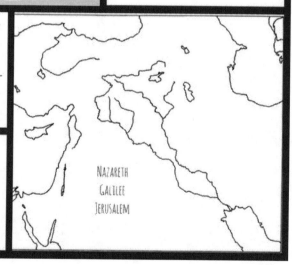

Nazareth
Galilee
Jerusalem

BIBLE FACTS

Jesus' Names, Verse 5
To the tune of "You Are My Sunshine"

Head of the Whole Church

And Heir of All Things,

The Captain of our Salvation,

Author and Finisher of our Faith, Door,

The Desire of Nations.

TIMELINE

Jesus feeds 5000,

Transfiguration,

Miracles abounding

J	R	P	T	R
-5	33	46-58	70	96

hymn

COME THOU ALMIGHTY KING
verse 1

Come, Thou almighty King,
Help us Thy Name to sing,
Help us to praise!
Father all glorious,
O'er all victorious,
Come and reign over us,
Ancient of Days!

I PRACTICED:

☆ ☆ ☆ ☆ ☆ ☆

M	T	W	T	F	S
O	U	E	H	R	A
N	E	D	U	I	T

CYCLE 2
Jesus feeds 5000
WEEK 5

1 Corinthians 13:5

It is not rude,
it is not self-seeking,
it is not easily
angered,
it keeps no record of
wrongs.

related stories

Matthew 14,
John 6, Mark 8

Vos New
Testament
Lessons 26, 30

Hurlbut Part 6
Lesson 19

Iota
I ι

Kappa
K κ

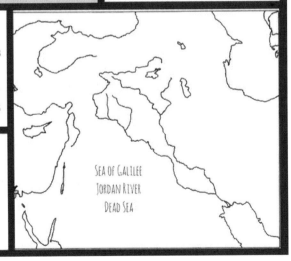

Sea of Galilee
Jordan River
Dead Sea

BIBLE FACTS
The Twelve Disciples

Peter, Andrew, James and John,

Fishermen of Capernaum,

Thomas and Saint Matthew too,

Philip and Bartholomew,

James, his brother Thaddeus,

Simon and the one called Judas,

Twelve Disciples, Jesus chose,

Called Apostles when He rose.

TIMELINE

Parables

Triumphal Entry

Olivet Discourse on

things to be

J	R	P	T	R
-5	33	46-58	70	96

hymn

COME THOU ALMIGHTY KING
verse 3

Come, Thou incarnate Word,

Gird on Thy mighty sword,

Our prayer attend!

Come and Thy people bless,

And give Thy word success,

Spirit of holiness,

On us descend.

I PRACTICED:
☆ ☆ ☆ ☆ ☆ ☆

M	T	W	T	F	S
O	U	E	H	R	A
N	E	D	U	I	T

CYCLE 2
Parables
WEEK 6

1 Corinthians 13:6-7

Love does not delight in evil but rejoices with the truth. It always protects, always trusts, always hopes, always perseveres.

related stories

Luke 10-20

Vos New Testament Lessons 22, 33, 37

Hurlbut Part 6 Lessons 15, 25, 27, 28

Lambda
Λ λ

Mu
M μ

Sea of Galilee
Bethsaida
Capernaum

BIBLE FACTS

The Twelve Disciples

Peter, Andrew, James and John,

Fishermen of Capernaum,

Thomas and Saint Matthew too,

Philip and Bartholomew,

James, his brother Thaddeus,

Simon and the one called Judas,

Twelve Disciples, Jesus chose,

Called Apostles when He rose.

TIMELINE

Last Passover

Crucifixion

Resurrection

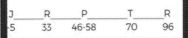

J	R	P	T	R
-5	33	46-58	70	96

hymn

COME THOU ALMIGHTY KING
verse 4

Come, holy Comforter,
Thy sacred witness bear,
In this glad hour;
Thou Who almighty art,
Now rule in every heart,
And ne'er from us depart,
Spirit of pow'r!

I PRACTICED:

☆ ☆ ☆ ☆ ☆ ☆

M	T	W	T	F	S
O	U	E	H	R	A
N	E	D	U	I	T

CYCLE 2
Last Passover
WEEK 7

1 Corinthians 13:8

Love never fails.
But where there
are prophecies,
they will cease;
where there are
tongues, they will
be stilled; where
there is knowledge,
it will pass away.

related stories

Mark 26, Luke 22

Vos New
Testament
Lessons 44, 45

Hurlbut Part 6
Lessons 33, 34

Nu
N ν

Xi
Ξ ξ

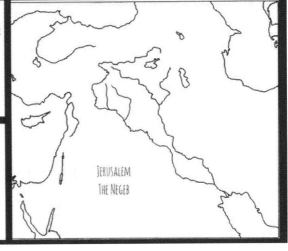

Jerusalem
The Negeb

BIBLE FACTS

The Twelve Disciples

Peter, Andrew, James and John,

Fishermen of Capernaum,

Thomas and Saint Matthew too,

Philip and Bartholomew,

James, his brother Thaddeus,

Simon and the one called Judas,

Twelve Disciples, Jesus chose,

Called Apostles when He rose.

TIMELINE

Ascension

Pentecost, Holy Spirit received

Peter preaches, 3,000 believe

J	R	P	T	R
-5	33	46-58	70	96

hymn

COME THOU ALMIGHTY KING
verse 5

To Thee, great One in Three,
Eternal praises be,
Hence, evermore;
Thy sov'reign majesty,
May we in glory see,
And to eternity,
Love and adore!

I PRACTICED:

☆ ☆ ☆ ☆ ☆ ☆

M	T	W	T	F	S
O	U	E	H	R	A
N	E	D	U	I	T

CYCLE 2
Ascension
WEEK 8

1 Corinthians 13:9-10

For we know in part and we prophesy in part, but when perfection comes, the imperfect disappears.

related stories

Luke 24, Acts 1

Vos New Testament Lessons 55, 56

Hurlbut Part 6 Lesson 38

Omicron
O o

Pi
Π π

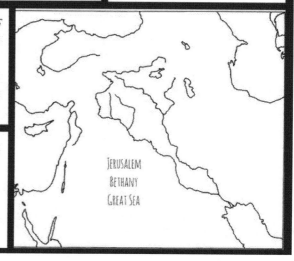

Jerusalem
Bethany
Great Sea

BIBLE FACTS

The Apostles' Creed
Part 1 of 4 Parts
Music used with permission from Jamie Soles

I believe in God, the Father Almighty,

Maker of heaven and earth;

And in Jesus Christ,

His only begotten Son, our Lord;

Who was conceived by the Holy Spirit,

TIMELINE

Stephen martyred

Conversion of Saul

Paul's first journey

J	R	P	T	R
-5	33	46-58	70	96

hymn

PRAISE TO THE LORD, THE ALMIGHTY
verse 1

Praise to the Lord,
the Almighty,
the King of creation!
O my soul, praise Him,
for He is thy health
and salvation!
All ye who hear,
now to His temple draw near;
Praise Him in glad adoration.

I PRACTICED:

☆ ☆ ☆ ☆ ☆ ☆

M	T	W	T	F	S
O	U	E	H	R	A
N	E	D	U	I	T

CYCLE 2
Stephen martyred
WEEK 9

1 Corinthians 13:11

When I was a child, I talked like a child, I thought like a child, I reasoned like a child. When I became a man, I put childish ways behind me.

related stories

Acts 7

Vos New Testament Lessons 61, 63

Hurlbut Part 7 Lesson 4

Rho
P ρ

Sigma
Σ σ

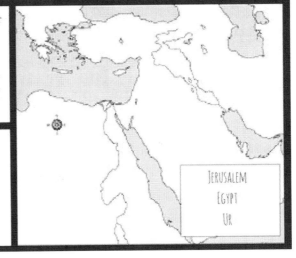

Jerusalem
Egypt
Ur

BIBLE FACTS

The Apostles' Creed
Part 2 of 4 Parts
Music used with permission from Jamie Soles

Born of the Virgin Mary,

Suffered under Pontius Pilate,

Was crucified, dead and buried;

He descended into hell;

The third day he rose again

from the dead;

He ascended into Heaven,

Jerusalem Council

Paul's Second Journey

Thessalonians, Galatians, Romans, Corinthians

J		R		P		T		R
-5		33		46-58		70		96

hymn

PRAISE TO THE LORD, THE ALMIGHTY
verse 2

Praise to the Lord,
Who o'er all things so
wonderfully reigneth,
Shelters thee under His wings,
Yea, so gladly sustaineth,
Hast thou not seen,
How thy desires e'er have been
Granted in what He ordaineth.

I PRACTICED:

☆ ☆ ☆ ☆ ☆ ☆

M	T	W	T	F	S
O	U	E	H	R	A
N	E	D	U	I	T

CYCLE 2
Jerusalem Council
WEEK 10

1 Corinthians 13:12

related stories

Acts 15

Vos New Testament Lessons 68, 69

Hurlbut Part 7 Lesson 10

For now we see but a poor reflection, as in a mirror; then we shall see face to face. Now I know in part; then I shall know fully, even as I am fully known.

Tau
T τ

Upsilon
Y υ

JERUSALEM
ANTIOCH
ATHENS

BIBLE FACTS

The Apostles' Creed
Part 3 of 4 Parts
Music used with permission from Jamie Soles

And sitteth at the right hand

of God the Father Almighty;

From thence He shall come to judge

the living and the dead.

I believe in the Holy Spirit;

TIMELINE

Paul sent to prison

Paul stands trial

Paul shipwrecked on an isle

J	R	P	T	R
-5	33	46-58	70	96

hymn

PRAISE TO THE LORD, THE ALMIGHTY
verse 3

Praise to the Lord,
who doth prosper thy work
and defend thee;
Surely His goodness and
mercy here daily attend thee;
Ponder anew
what the Almighty can do,
If with His love
He befriend thee.

I PRACTICED:
☆ ☆ ☆ ☆ ☆

M	T	W	T	F	S
O	U	E	H	R	A
N	E	D	U	I	T

CYCLE 2
Paul sent to prison
WEEK 11

1 Corinthians 13:13

And now these three remain: faith, hope and love. But the greatest of these is love.

related stories
Acts 16, 27

Vos New Testament Lesson 91

Hurlbut Part 7 Lesson 16, 17

Phi
Φ φ

Chi
Χ χ

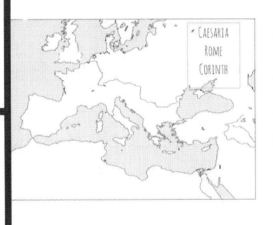
CAESARIA
ROME
CORINTH

BIBLE FACTS

The Apostles' Creed
Part 4 of 4 Parts
Music used with permission from Jamie Soles

The holy catholic Church,

The communion of saints,

The forgiveness of sins;

The resurrection of the body,

And life everlasting. Amen.

TIMELINE

Paul writes more letters from prison

Titus sacks the Temple

Revelation vision

J	R	P	T	R
-5	33	46-58	70	96

hymn

PRAISE TO THE LORD,
THE ALMIGHTY
verse 6

Praise to the Lord, oh, let all
that is in me adore Him!
All that hath life and breath,
come now with praises
before Him;
Let the Amen
sound from His people again,
Gladly for aye we adore Him.

I PRACTICED:
☆ ☆ ☆ ☆ ☆ ☆
M T W T F S
O U E H R A
N E D U I T

CYCLE 2
Paul's Prison Letters
WEEK 12

REVIEW!

related stories

Ephesians,
Philippians,
Colossians,
Philemon

Hurlbut Part 7
Lesson 19

Psi
Ψ ψ

Omega
Ω ω

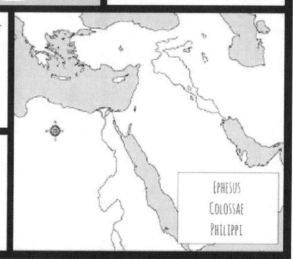

EPHESUS
COLOSSAE
PHILIPPI

Old Testament Timeline

Creation, Fall, Cain and Abel,
Flood, Job, Tower of Babel,
Abraham, Ishmael,
Sodom and Gomorrah, Isaac as Well.

Jacob and Esau, Israel's Tribes,
Joseph in Egypt, Moses' Life,
Burning Bush and Plagues in Egypt,
Exodus and Ten Commandments.

Desert, Ark, Feasts, Tabernacle,
Joshua's Conquest, Judges Rule,
Ruth and Boaz, King Saul's Reign,
David's Kingdom, Psalms, Covenant.

Solomon's Temple, Kingdom Divides,
Ahab and Elijah on the North Side,
Hezekiah and Isaiah in the South,
Israel Falls to Assyria's Clout.

Jeremiah and Ezekiel Warn Judah,
Judah Falls To Babylon,
Temple Ruined
Daniel in the Exile, Cyrus' Decree,
Exiles Return, Temple Rebuilding.

Esther Saves the Jews,
Nehemiah Builds the Wall,
Malachi Foretells John the Baptist's Call,
Maccabean Period Ends Here,
No Word from God for 400 Years.

Hymns

It Is Well
Come, Thou Almighty King
Praise to the Lord, the Almighty

Days of Creation

DAY 1: Day and Night
DAY 2: Sky and Water
DAY 3: Land and Plants
DAY 4: Sun, Moon and Stars
DAY 5: Birds and Fish
DAY 6: Animals and Man
DAY 7: God rested

Psalm 1

Blessed is the man
who does not walk in the
counsel of the wicked
or stand in the way of sinners
or sit in the seat of mockers.
2 But his delight is in the law of
the Lord,
and on his law
he meditates day and night.
3 He is like a tree planted by
streams of water,
which yields its fruit in season
and whose leaf does not wither.
Whatever he does prospers.
4 Not so the wicked!
They are like chaff
that the wind blows away.
5 Therefore the wicked will not
stand in the judgment,
nor sinners in the assembly of
the righteous.
6 For the Lord watches over the
way of the righteous,
but the way of the wicked will
perish.

Abraham's Descendants

Abraham and Sarah,
Sarah, Sarah,
Abraham and Sarah
had baby Isaac.

Isaac and Rebekah,
Rebekah, Rebekah,
Isaac and Rebekah had
Jacob and Esau.

Jacob and Rachel,
Leah, Bilhah,
And the last one Zilpah
Had the Sons of Israel.

Hebrew Alphabet

Jacob's Descendants

Reuben, Simeon, Levi,
Judah,
Issachar, Zebulon, Joseph,
Benjamin,
Dan, Naphtali, Gad and
Asher,
Sons of Israel

New Testament Timeline

John the Baptist, Messiah Is Born,
Shepherds and Magi Visit the Lord,
Flight into Egypt, Herod's Slaughter,
Boy Jesus at the Temple,
Baptism at the Jordan.

Temptation in the Desert,
Disciples' Call, Cana Wedding,
Jubilee Inaugural
Jesus Clears the Temple,
Ministry Begins,
Meets Nicodemus and the Samaritan.

Sermon on the Mount,
Jesus Feeds 5000,
Transfiguration, Miracles Abounding,
Parables, Triumphal Entry,
Olivet Discourse on Things to Be.

Last Passover, Crucifixion,
Resurrection, Ascension,
Pentecost, Holy Spirit Received,
Peter Preaches, 3000 Believe.

Stephen Martyred, Conversion of Saul,
Paul's First Journey, Jerusalem Council,
Paul's Second Journey, Thessalonians,
Romans, Galatians, Corinthians.

Paul Sent to Prison, Paul Stands Trial,
Paul Shipwrecked on an Isle,
Paul Writes More Letters from Prison,
Titus Sacks the Temple,
Revelation Vision.

Names of Jesus

Alpha, Omega, Lion of Judah,
Messiah, Shepherd of the Sheep,
Immanuel, Friend, Lord of Glory,
Our Passover, Our Great High Priest.

Prophet, Lord, Savior,
And King of all Kings,
Mediator 'tween God and Men,
Rock, Vine, Bread of Life,
And the Good Shepherd,
The Firstborn from the Dead.

Only Begotten of the Father, Rabbi,
The Seed of Abraham, The Last Adam,
The Word Become Flesh,
Son of God, the Son of Man.

The Lord of all Lords, God's Pascal Lamb,
Morning Star and Chief Cornerstone,
Light of the World,
Bread Come Down from Heaven,
Redeemer, Master, God's Holy One

Head of the Whole Church
And Heir of All Things,
The Captain of our Salvation,
Author and Finisher of our Faith, Door,
The Desire of Nations.

Hymns

Amazing Grace
The Church's One Foundation
Holy, Holy, Holy

Greek Alphabet

The Apostles' Creed

I believe in God,
the Father Almighty,
Maker of heaven and earth;
And in Jesus Christ,
His only begotten Son, our Lord;
Who was conceived
by the Holy Spirit,
Born of the Virgin Mary,
Suffered under Pontius Pilate,
Was crucified, dead and buried;
He descended into hell;
The third day he rose
again from the dead;
He ascended into Heaven,
And sitteth at the right hand
of God the Father Almighty;
From thence He shall come to
judge the living and the dead.
I believe in the Holy Spirit;
the holy catholic Church,
the communion of saints,
the forgiveness of sins;
The resurrection of the body,
and life everlasting. Amen.

1 Corinthians 13

If I speak in the tongues of men or
of angels, but have not love, I am
only a resounding gong or a
clanging cymbal. If I have the gift
of prophecy and can fathom all
mysteries and all knowledge, and
if I have a faith that can move
mountains, but have not love, I am
nothing. If I give all I possess to the
poor and surrender my body to
the flames, but have not love, I
gain nothing.

Love is patient, love is kind. It does
not envy, it does not boast, it is not
proud. It is not rude, it is not self-
seeking, it is not easily angered, it
keeps no record of wrongs. Love
does not delight in evil but rejoices
with the truth. It always protects,
always trusts, always hopes, always
perseveres.

Love never fails. But where there
are prophecies, they will cease;
where there are tongues, they will
be stilled; where there is
knowledge, it will pass away. For
we know in part and we prophesy
in part, but when perfection
comes, the imperfect disappears.
When I was a child, I talked like a
child, I thought like a child, I
reasoned like a child. When I
became a man, I put childish ways
behind me. Now we
see but a poor reflection as in a
mirror; then we shall see face to
face. Now I know in part; then I
shall know fully, even as I am fully
known.

And now these three remain: faith,
hope and love. But the greatest of
these is love.

The 12 Disciples

Peter, Andrew, James and John,
Fishermen of Capernaum,
Thomas and Saint Matthew too,
Philip and Bartholomew,
James, his brother Thaddeus,
Simon and the one called Judas,
Twelve Disciples, Jesus chose,
Called Apostles when He rose.

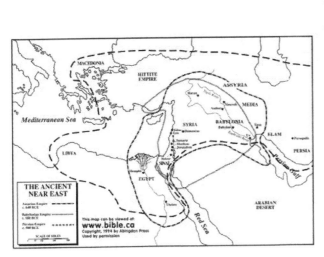

THE ANCIENT
NEAR EAST

SCALE OF MILES

Israel
at the
Time of Christ
30 AD

SCALE OF MILES

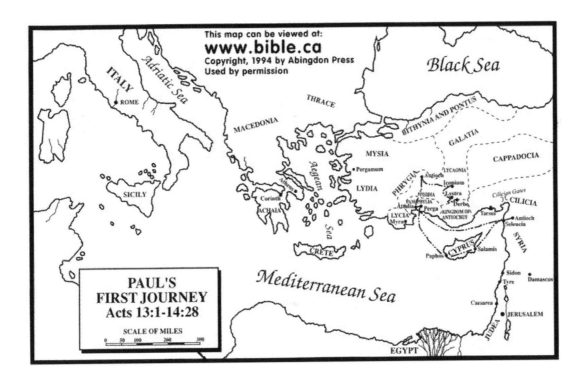

**PAUL'S
FIRST JOURNEY
Acts 13:1-14:28**

SCALE OF MILES
0   50   100   200   300

Classical
Sunday School

FAMILY DRILL BOOK
CYCLES 3 & 4

To learn more about Classical education, and for
great tips on using this Drill Book, go to
StrongHappyFamily.org.

BIBLE FACTS

OLD TESTAMENT BOOKS

Genesis, Exodus, Leviticus

Numbers, Deuteronomy

Joshua, Judges, Ruth

1 Samuel, 2 Samuel

TIMELINE

Creation

Fall

Cain and Abel

hymn

BE THOU MY VISION
verse 1

Be Thou my Vision,
O Lord of my heart;
Naught be all else to me,
save that Thou art.
Thou my best Thought,
by day or by night,
Waking or sleeping,
Thy presence my light.

I PRACTICED:

☆ ☆ ☆ ☆ ☆ ☆

M	T	W	T	F	S
O	U	E	H	R	A
N	E	D	U	I	T

CYCLE 3

FALL

WEEK 1

ISAIAH 53:1

Who has believed our message and to whom has the arm of the Lord been revealed?

related stories

Genesis 3

Vos Old Testament Lessons 5-7

Hurlbut Part 1 Lesson 1

Aleph
א

Bet
ב

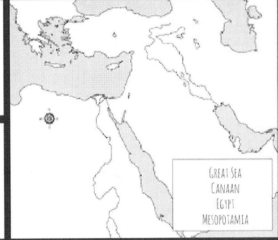

GREAT SEA
CANAAN
EGYPT
MESOPOTAMIA

BIBLE FACTS

OLD TESTAMENT BOOKS

1 Kings, 2 Kings

1 Chronicles, 2 Chronicles

Ezra, Nehemiah

Esther, Job

Psalms, Proverbs

TIMELINE

Flood

Job

Tower of Babel

hymn

BE THOU MY VISION
verse 2

Be Thou my Wisdom,
and Thou my true Word;
I ever with Thee
and Thou with me, Lord;
Thou my great Father,
I Thy true son;
Thou in me dwelling,
and I with Thee one.

I PRACTICED:

☆ ☆ ☆ ☆ ☆ ☆
M T W T F S
O U E H R A
N E D U I T

CYCLE 3
JOB
WEEK 2

ISAIAH 53:2

He grew up before him like a tender shoot, and like a root out of dry ground. He had no beauty or majesty to attract us to him, nothing in his appearance that we should desire him.

related stories

Job 1-42

Hurlbut Part 1
Lesson 35

Gimel
ג

Dalet
ד

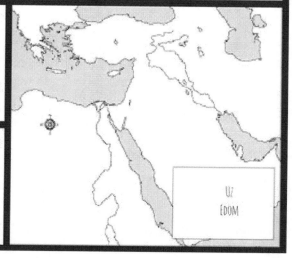

Uz
Edom

BIBLE FACTS

OLD TESTAMENT BOOKS

Ecclesiastes,
Song of Solomon
Isaiah, Jeremiah
Lamentations, Ezekiel
Daniel, Hosea
Joel, Amos, Obadiah

TIMELINE

Abraham

Ishmael

Sodom and
Gomorrah

A ___ M ___ D ___ E
2000   1500   1000   500

hymn

BE THOU MY VISION
verse 4
Riches I heed not,
nor man's empty praise,
Thou mine Inheritance,
now and always:
Thou and Thou only,
first in my heart,
High King of Heaven,
my Treasure Thou art.

I PRACTICED:

☆ ☆ ☆ ☆ ☆ ☆

M	T	W	T	F	S
O	U	E	H	R	A
N	E	D	U	I	T

CYCLE 3

ISHMAEL

WEEK 3

ISAIAH 53:3

He was despised and
rejected by men, a man
of sorrows, and familiar
with suffering. Like one
from whom men hide
their faces he was
despised, and
we esteemed him not.

related stories

Genesis 16-17

Vos Old
Testament
Lessons 13, 15

Hurlbut Part 1
Lesson 9

He
ה

Vav
ו

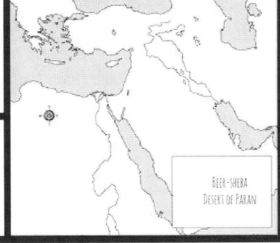

BEER-SHEBA
DESERT OF PARAN

BIBLE FACTS

OLD TESTAMENT BOOKS

Jonah, Micah, Nahum

Habakkuk, Zephaniah

Haggai, Zechariah

Malachi

TIMELINE

Isaac as well

Jacob and Esau

Israel's tribes

A	M	D	E
2000	1500	1000	500

hymn

BE THOU MY VISION
verse 5
High King of Heaven,
my victory won,
May I reach Heaven's joys,
O bright Heaven's Sun!
Heart of my own heart,
whatever befall,
Still be my Vision,
O Ruler of all.

I PRACTICED:

☆ ☆ ☆ ☆ ☆ ☆

M	T	W	T	F	S
O	U	E	H	R	A
N	E	D	U	I	T

CYCLE 3
JACOB AND ESAU
WEEK 4

ISAIAH 53:4

Surely he took up our infirmities and carried our sorrows, yet we considered him stricken by God, smitten by him, and afflicted.

related stories

Genesis 32

Vos Old Testament Lessons 18-20

Hurlbut Part 1 Lessons 12, 14

Zayin
ז

Het
ח

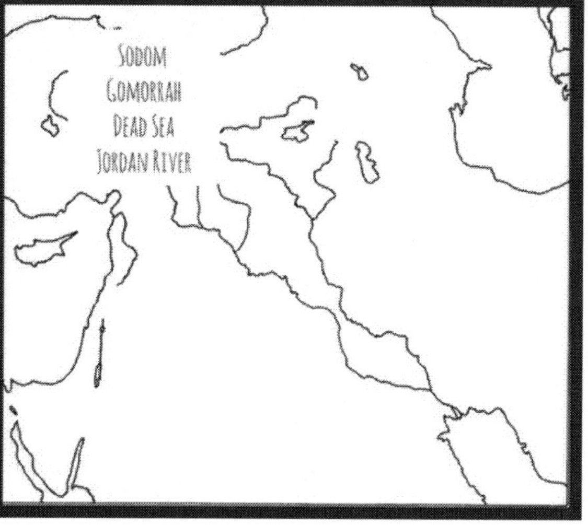

SODOM
GOMORRAH
DEAD SEA
JORDAN RIVER

BIBLE FACTS

The Ten Commandments
To the Tune of "The 12 Days of Christmas"

1. I am your God; have no gods before Me.
2. Do not worship idols.
3. Don't take My name in vain.
4. Keep the sabbath holy.
5. Honor your father and mother.
6. Do not murder.
7. Don't commit adultery.
8. Do not steal.
9. Don't bear false witness.
10. Do not covet.

I PRACTICED:

☆ ☆ ☆ ☆ ☆ ☆

M	T	W	T	F	S
O	U	E	H	R	A
N	E	D	U	I	T

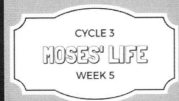

CYCLE 3

MOSES' LIFE

WEEK 5

TIMELINE

Joseph in Egypt

Moses' Life

Burning bush
and plagues in
Egypt

A	M	D	E
2000	1500	1000	500

hymn

ALL CREATURES
OF OUR GOD AND KING
verse 1

All creatures of our God and King,
lift up your voice and with us sing:
alleluia, alleluia!
O burning sun with golden beam,
and shining moon
with silver gleam,
O praise him, O praise him,
alleluia, alleluia, alleluia!

ISAIAH 53:5

But he was pierced for our
transgressions,
he was crushed for our
iniquities;
the punishment that brought
us peace was upon him,
and by his wounds we are
healed.

related stories

Genesis
Exodus 2-40

Vos Old
Testament
Lesson 32

Hurlbut Part 1
Lessons 20, 34

Tet
ט

Yod
י

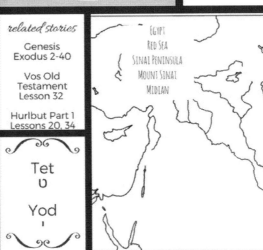

EGYPT
RED SEA
SINAI PENINSULA
MOUNT SINAI
MIDIAN

BIBLE FACTS
The Ten Commandments
To the tune of "The 12 Days of Christmas"

1. I am your God; have no gods before Me.
2. Do not worship idols.
3. Don't take My name in vain.
4. Keep the sabbath holy.
5. Honor your father and mother.
6. Do not murder.
7. Don't commit adultery.
8. Do not steal.
9. Don't bear false witness.
10. Do not covet.

TIMELINE

Exodus and 10 Commandments

Desert, Ark, Feasts, Tabernacle

Joshua's Conquest

_A_	_M_	_D_	_E_
2000	1500	1000	500

hymn

ALL CREATURES
OF OUR GOD AND KING
verse 2

O rushing wind
so wild and strong,
white clouds that sail
in heaven along,
alleluia, alleluia!
New rising dawn
in praise rejoice;
you lights of evening
find a voice:
O praise him, O praise him,
alleluia, alleluia, alleluia!

I PRACTICED:

☆ ☆ ☆ ☆ ☆ ☆

M	T	W	T	F	S
O	U	E	H	R	A
N	E	D	U	I	T

CYCLE 3
DESERT, ARK, FEASTS, TABERNACLE
WEEK 6

ISAIAH 53:6

We all, like sheep, have gone astray, each of us has turned to his own way; and the Lord has laid on him the iniquity of us all.

related stories

Exodus 16-40

Vos Old Testament Lessons 40-45

Hurlbut Part 1 Lessons 27-33

Kaf
כ
ך

Lamed
ל

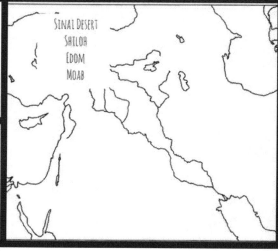

BIBLE FACTS

The Ten Commandments

To the tune of "The Twelve Days of Christmas"

1. I am your God; have no gods before Me.
2. Do not worship idols.
3. Don't take My name in vain.
4. Keep the sabbath holy.
5. Honor your father and mother.
6. Do not murder.
7. Don't commit adultery.
8. Do not steal.
9. Don't bear false witness.
10. Do not covet.

TIMELINE

Judges rule

Ruth and Boaz

King Saul's reign

A	M	D	E
2000	1500	1000	500

hymn

ALL CREATURES OF OUR GOD AND KING
verse 5

All you who are of tender heart,
forgiving others, take your part;
alleluia, alleluia!
All you who pain
and sorrow bear,
praise God and
on him cast your care;
O praise him, O praise him,
alleluia, alleluia, alleluia!

I PRACTICED:

☆ ☆ ☆ ☆ ☆ ☆

M	T	W	T	F	S
O	U	E	H	R	A
N	E	D	U	I	T

CYCLE 3
RUTH AND BOAZ
WEEK 7

ISAIAH 53:7

He was oppressed and afflicted, yet he did not open his mouth;
he was led like a lamb to the slaughter, and as a sheep
before her shearers is silent, so he did not open his mouth.

related stories

Ruth 1-4

Vos Old Testament Lesson 64

Hurlbut Part 2 Lesson 14

Mem
ה
ם

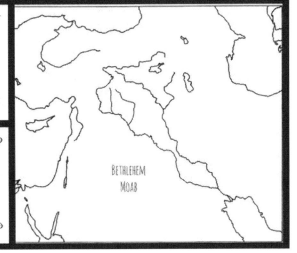

BETHLEHEM
MOAB

BIBLE FACTS

The Ten Commandments

To the tune of "The 12 Days of Christmas"

1. I am your God; have no gods before Me.
2. Do not worship idols.
3. Don't take My name in vain.
4. Keep the sabbath holy.
5. Honor your father and mother.
6. Do not murder.
7. Don't commit adultery.
8. Do not steal.
9. Don't bear false witness.
10. Do not covet.

TIMELINE

David's Kingdom

Psalms,
David's Covenant

Solomon's Temple,
Kingdom divides

A	M	D	E
2000	1500	1000	500

hymn

ALL CREATURES OF OUR GOD AND KING
verse 6

Let all things their Creator bless,
and worship him
in humbleness,
alleluia, alleluia!
Praise, praise the Father,
praise the Son,
and praise the Spirit,
Three in One:
O praise him, O praise him,
alleluia, alleluia, alleluia!

I PRACTICED:

☆ ☆ ☆ ☆ ☆ ☆

M	T	W	T	F	S
O	U	E	H	R	A
N	E	D	U	I	T

CYCLE 3
PSALMS
DAVID'S COVENANT
WEEK 8

ISAIAH 53:8

By oppression and judgment he was taken away. And who can speak of his descendants? For he was cut off from the land of the living; for the transgression of my people he was stricken.

related stories

Psalms 1-150
2 Samuel 7

Vos Old Testament Lessons 72-73

Hurlbut Part 3 Lessons 10, 11, 13

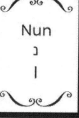

Nun

ו

ן

Jerusalem
Jordan River
Dead Sea

BIBLE FACTS

The Judges

To the tune of "Jesus Loves Me"

Othniel, Ehud, Shamgar,

Deborah, Gideon, Abimelech, Tola, Jair,

Jephthah, Ibzan, Elon, Abdon,

Samson, Eli, Samuel

Judges of Israel, Judges of Israel,

Judges of Israel,

Because God was their King.

TIMELINE

Ahab and Elijah on the north side

Hezekiah and Isaiah in the South

Israel falls to Assyria's clout

A	M	D	E
2000	1500	1000	500

hymn

ALL HAIL THE POWER
verse 1

All hail the power of Jesus' name!
Let angels prostrate fall.
Bring forth the royal diadem,
and crown him Lord of all.
Bring forth the royal diadem,
and crown him Lord of all!

I PRACTICED:

☆ ☆ ☆ ☆ ☆ ☆

M	T	W	T	F	S
O	U	E	H	R	A
N	E	D	U	I	T

CYCLE 3
HEZEKIAH AND ISAIAH
IN THE SOUTH
WEEK 9

ISAIAH 53:9

He was assigned a grave with the wicked, and with the rich in his death, though he had done no violence, nor was any deceit in his mouth.

related stories

Isaiah 1-66
2 Kings 18-20

Vos Old Testament Lessons 88, 90-93, 95-97

Hurlbut Part 5 Lessons 1-5

Samekh
ס
Ayin
ע

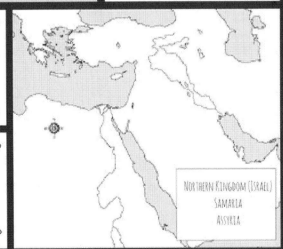

Northern Kingdom (Israel)
Samaria
Assyria

BIBLE FACTS

The Judges

To the tune of "Jesus Loves Me"

Othniel, Ehud, Shamgar,

Deborah, Gideon, Abimelech, Tola, Jair,

Jephthah, Ibzan, Elon, Abdon,

Samson, Eli, Samuel

Judges of Israel, Judges of Israel,

Judges of Israel,

Because God was their King.

TIMELINE

Jeremiah and Ezekiel warn Judah

Judah falls to Babylon, Temple ruined

Daniel in the Exile

_A_	_M_	_D_	_E_
2000	1500	1000	500

hymn

ALL HAIL THE POWER
verse 2

O seed of Israel's chosen race
now ransomed from the fall,
hail him who saves you
by his grace,
and crown him Lord of all.
Hail him who saves you
by his grace,
and crown him Lord of all!

I PRACTICED:

☆ ☆ ☆ ☆ ☆ ☆

M	T	W	T	F	S
O	U	E	H	R	A
N	E	D	U	I	T

CYCLE 3
JUDAH FALLS TO BABYLON
TEMPLE RUINED
WEEK 10

ISAIAH 53:10

Yet it was the Lord's will to crush him and cause him to suffer, and though the Lord makes his life a guilt offering, he will see his offspring and prolong his days, and the will of the Lord will prosper in his hand.

related stories

2 Chronicles 36

Vos Old Testament Lessons 98-99

Hurlbut Part 5 Lessons 6-7

Pe
פ
ף
Tsadi
צ
ץ

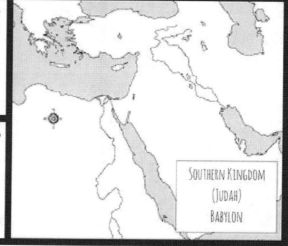

SOUTHERN KINGDOM (JUDAH)
BABYLON

BIBLE FACTS

The Judges

To the tune of "Jesus Loves Me"

Othniel, Ehud, Shamgar,

Deborah, Gideon, Abimelech, Tola, Jair,

Jephthah, Ibzan, Elon, Abdon,

Samson, Eli, Samuel

Judges of Israel, Judges of Israel,

Judges of Israel,

Because God was their King.

TIMELINE

Cyrus' decree
Exiles return

Temple rebuilding

Esther saves the Jews

A	M	D	E
2000	1500	1000	500

hymn

ALL HAIL THE POWER
verse 3

Let every tongue
and every tribe
responsive to his call,
to him all majesty ascribe,
and crown him Lord of all.
To him all majesty ascribe,
and crown him Lord of all!

I PRACTICED:

☆ ☆ ☆ ☆ ☆ ☆

M	T	W	T	F	S
O	U	E	H	R	A
N	E	D	U	I	T

CYCLE 3
TEMPLE REBUILDING
WEEK 11

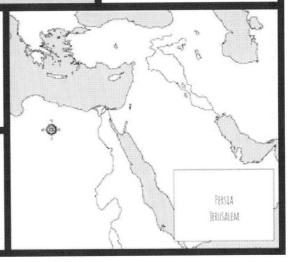

ISAIAH 53:11

After the suffering of his soul,he will see the light of life and be satisfied; by his knowledge my righteous servant will justify many, and he will bear their iniquities.

related stories

Haggai 1-2

Vos Old Testament Lesson 109

Hurlbut Part 5 Lesson 14

Qof
ק

Resh
ר

PERSIA
JERUSALEM

BIBLE FACTS

The Judges

To the tune of "Jesus Loves Me"

Othniel, Ehud, Shamgar,

Deborah, Gideon, Abimelech, Tola, Jair,

Jephthah, Ibzan, Elon, Abdon,

Samson, Eli, Samuel

Judges of Israel, Judges of Israel,

Judges of Israel,

Because God was their King.

TIMELINE

Nehemiah builds the wall

Malachi foretells John the Baptist's call

Maccabean period ends here, no word from God for 400 years

A	M	D	E
2000	1500	1000	500

hymn

ALL HAIL THE POWER
verse 4

Oh, that with yonder sacred throng
we at his feet may fall!
We'll join the everlasting song
and crown him Lord of all.
We'll join the everlasting song
and crown him Lord of all.

I PRACTICED:

☆ ☆ ☆ ☆ ☆ ☆

M	T	W	T	F	S
O	U	E	H	R	A
N	E	D	U	I	T

CYCLE 3
MALACHI
WEEK 12

ISAIAH 53:12

Therefore I will give him a portion among the great, and he will divide the spoils with the strong, because he poured out his life unto death, and was numbered with the transgressors. For he bore the sin of many, and made intercession for the transgressors.

related stories

Malachi 3-4

Vos New Testament Lesson 1

Hurlbut Part 5 Lesson 18

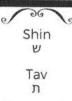

Shin
ש

Tav
ת

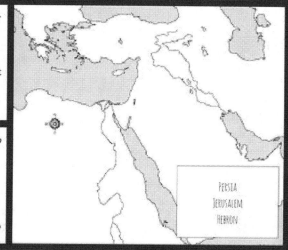

PERSIA
JERUSALEM
HEBRON

BIBLE FACTS
New Testament Books

Matthew

Mark

Luke

John

Acts

Romans

John the Baptist

Messiah is born

Shepherds and
Magi visit the Lord

J	R	P	T	R
-5	33	46-58	70	96

hymn

BLESSED ASSURANCE
verse 1

Blessed assurance: Jesus is mine!
Oh, what a foretaste
of glory divine!
Heir of salvation, purchase of God,
born of his Spirit,
washed in his blood.

Refrain:
This is my story, this is my song,
praising my Savior all the day long;
this is my story, this is my song,
praising my Savior all the day long.

I PRACTICED:

☆ ☆ ☆ ☆ ☆ ☆

M	T	W	T	F	S
O	U	E	H	R	A
N	E	D	U	I	T

CYCLE 4
MESSIAH IS BORN
WEEK 1

COLOSSIANS 1:15

He is the image of
the invisible God, the
firstborn over all
creation.

related stories

Luke 2

Vos New
Testament
Lessons 2-4

Hurlbut Part 6
Lesson 2

Alpha
A α

Beta
B β

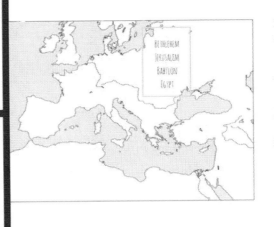

BIBLE FACTS
New Testament Books

1 Corinthians

2 Corinthians

Galatians

Ephesians

Philippians

Colossians

1 Thessalonians

2 Thessalonians

TIMELINE

Flight into Egypt
Herod's Slaughter

Boy Jesus at the
Temple

Baptism at the
Jordan

J____R____P____T____R
-5   33   46-58   70   96

hymn

BLESSED ASSURANCE
verse 2

Perfect submission,
perfect delight,
visions of rapture
now burst on my sight;
angels descending
bring from above
echoes of mercy, whispers of love.

Refrain:
This is my story, this is my song,
praising my Savior all the day long;
this is my story, this is my song,
praising my Savior all the day long.

I PRACTICED:

☆ ☆ ☆ ☆ ☆ ☆

M	T	W	T	F	S
O	U	E	H	R	A
N	E	D	U	I	T

CYCLE 4
BOY JESUS
AT THE TEMPLE
WEEK 2

COLOSSIANS 1:16a

For by him
all things were
created:
things in heaven
and on earth,
visible and
invisible,

related stories

Luke 2

Vos New
Testament
Lesson 6

Hurlbut Part 6
Lesson 4

Gamma
Γ γ

Delta
Δ δ

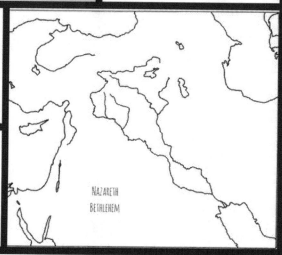

Nazareth
Bethlehem

BIBLE FACTS
New Testament Books

1 Timothy

2 Timothy

Titus

Philemon

Hebrews

James

1 Peter

2 Peter

TIMELINE

Temptation in the desert

Disciples' Call

Cana Wedding
Jubilee Inaugural

J	R	P	T	R
-5	33	46-58	70	96

hymn

BLESSED ASSURANCE
verse 3

Perfect submission, all is at rest,
I in my Savior am happy and blest;
watching and waiting,
looking above,
filled with his goodness,
lost in his love.

Refrain:
This is my story, this is my song,
praising my Savior all the day long;
this is my story, this is my song,
praising my Savior all the day long.

I PRACTICED:
☆ ☆ ☆ ☆ ☆ ☆

M	T	W	T	F	S
O	U	E	H	R	A
N	E	D	U	I	T

CYCLE 4
DISCIPLES' CALL
WEEK 3

COLOSSIANS 1:16b

whether thrones or
powers or rulers
or authorities;
all things
were created by him
and for him.

related stories

Matthew 4
Mark 1

Vos New
Testament
Lesson 8

Hurlbut Part 6
Lesson 6, 13

Epsilon
E ε

Zeta
Z ζ

Capernaum
Galilee
Sea of Galilee

BIBLE FACTS
NEW TESTAMENT BOOKS

1 John

2 John

3 John

Jude

Revelation

Jesus clears the Temple, Ministry begins

Meets Nicodemus and the Samaritan

Sermon on the Mount

J	R	P	T	R
-5	33	46-58	70	96

hymn

WHEN I SURVEY THE WONDROUS CROSS
verse 1

When I survey
the wondrous cross
on which the
Prince of glory died,
my richest gain
I count but loss,
and pour contempt
on all my pride.

I PRACTICED:
☆ ☆ ☆ ☆ ☆ ☆

M	T	W	T	F	S
O	U	E	H	R	A
N	E	D	U	I	T

CYCLE 4
JESUS MEETS NICODEMUS
AND THE SAMARITAN WOMAN
WEEK 4

COLOSSIANS 1:17

He is before all
things,
and in him
all things
hold together.

related stories

John 3-4

Vos New
Testament
Lessons 12, 13

Hurlbut Part 6
Lesson 8

Eta
H η

Theta
Θ θ

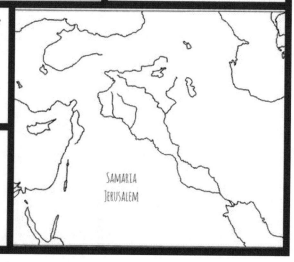

SAMARIA
JERUSALEM

BIBLE FACTS
The Fruit of the Spirit
To the tune of "Have You Ever Seen a Lassie?"

The fruit of the Spirit is

love, joy, peace, patience,

kindness, goodness, faithfulness,

gentleness, self-control.

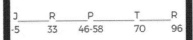

TIMELINE

Jesus feeds 5000,

Transfiguration,

Miracles abounding

J	R	P	T	R
-5	33	46-58	70	96

hymn

WHEN I SURVEY THE
WONDROUS CROSS
verse 2
Forbid it, Lord,
that I should boast
save in the death
of Christ, my God!
All the vain things
that charm me most,
I sacrifice them
through his blood.

I PRACTICED:
☆ ☆ ☆ ☆ ☆ ☆

M	T	W	T	F	S
O	U	E	H	R	A
N	E	D	U	I	T

CYCLE 4
TRANSFIGURATION
WEEK 5

COLOSSIANS 1:18

And he is
the head of the body,
the church;
he is the beginning
and the firstborn
from among the dead,
so that in everything
he might have the
supremacy.

related stories
Matthew 17,
Luke 9

Vos New
Testament
Lessons 31, 32

Hurlbut Part 6
Lesson 21

Iota
I ι

Kappa
K κ

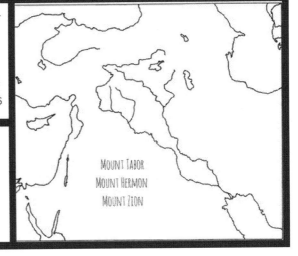

Mount Tabor
Mount Hermon
Mount Zion

BIBLE FACTS
The Fruit of the Spirit
To the tune of "Have You Ever seen a Lassie?"

The fruit of the Spirit is

love, joy, peace, patience,

kindness, goodness, faithfulness,

gentleness, self-control.

TIMELINE

Parables

Triumphal Entry

Olivet Discourse on

things to be

J	R	P	T	R
-5	33	46-58	70	96

hymn

WHEN I SURVEY THE
WONDROUS CROSS
verse 3
See, from his head,
his hands, his feet,
sorrow and love
flow mingled down.
Did e'er such love
and sorrow meet,
or thorns compose
so rich a crown?

I PRACTICED:

☆ ☆ ☆ ☆ ☆ ☆

M	T	W	T	F	S
O	U	E	H	R	A
N	E	D	U	I	T

CYCLE 4
TRIUMPHAL ENTRY
WEEK 6

COLOSSIANS 1:19

For God was
pleased to have all
his fullness dwell in
him.

related stories
Mark 11
Matthew 21

Vos New
Testament
Lesson 41

Hurlbut Part 6
Lesson 30

Lambda
Λ λ

Mu
M μ

Jerusalem
Bethany

BIBLE FACTS

The Fruit of the Spirit
To the tune of "Have You Ever seen a Lassie?"

The fruit of the Spirit is

love, joy, peace, patience,

kindness, goodness,

faithfulness, gentleness,

self-control.

TIMELINE

Last Passover

Crucifixion

Resurrection

J		R		P		T		R
-5		33		46-58		70		96

hymn

WHEN I SURVEY THE WONDROUS CROSS
verse 4

Were the whole realm
of nature mine,
that were a present
far too small.
Love so amazing,
so divine,
demands my soul,
my life, my all.

I PRACTICED:

☆ ☆ ☆ ☆ ☆ ☆

M	T	W	T	F	S
O	U	E	H	R	A
N	E	D	U	I	T

CYCLE 4
CRUCIFIXION
WEEK 7

COLOSSIANS 1:20

and through him
to reconcile to
himself all things,
whether
things on earth or
things in heaven,
by making peace
through his blood,
shed on the cross.

related stories

Matthew 27,
Luke 23, John 19

Vos New
Testament
Lessons 46-51

Hurlbut Part 6
Lessons 35, 36

Nu
N ν

Xi
Ξ ξ

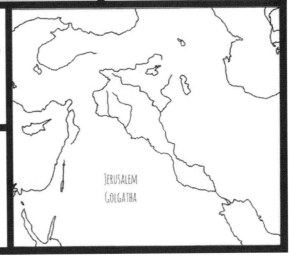

Jerusalem
Golgatha

BIBLE FACTS

Prophecies About Jesus

To the tune of "The Battle Hymn of the Republic," verse 1

The Bible prophesies about the coming of the Lord,

Micah 5 says Bethlehem is where He'll be born,

The virgin will give birth, Isaiah 7 has sworn

Messiah is born!

Refrain:

Jesus of the line of Abraham,

Jesus of the line of Isaac,

Jesus of the line of Jacob,

Born of Judah's line.

TIMELINE

Ascension

Pentecost, Holy Spirit received

Peter preaches, 3,000 believe

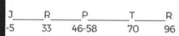

J	R	P	T	R
-5	33	46-58	70	96

hymn

O WORSHIP THE KING
verse 1

O worship the King
all-glorious above,
O gratefully sing his power
and his love:
our shield and defender,
the Ancient of Days,
pavilioned in splendor
and girded with praise.

I PRACTICED:

☆ ☆ ☆ ☆ ☆ ☆

M	T	W	T	F	S
O	U	E	H	R	A
N	E	D	U	I	T

CYCLE 4

PENTECOST

WEEK 8

COLOSSIANS 1:21

Once you were alienated from God and were enemies in your minds because of your evil behavior.

related stories

Acts 2

Vos New Testament Lessons 57

Hurlbut Part 7 Lesson 1

Omicron

O o

Pi

Π π

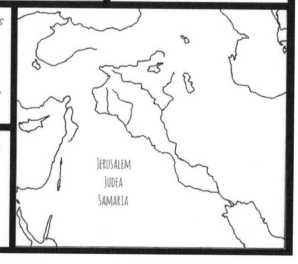

Jerusalem
Judea
Samaria

BIBLE FACTS

Prophecies about Jesus
To the tune of "The Battle Hymn of the Republic," verse 2

Second Samuel 7 says he'll sit on David's throne,
Hosea 11 says to Egypt He'll have flown.
Isaiah 7: by "Immanuel" he'll be known,
Messiah is shown.

Refrain:
Jesus of the line of Abraham,
Jesus of the line of Isaac,
Jesus of the line of Jacob,
Born of Judah's line.

TIMELINE

Stephen martyred

Conversion of Saul

Paul's first journey

J	R	P	T	R
-5	33	46-58	70	96

hymn

O WORSHIP THE KING
verse 2

O tell of his might
and sing of his grace,
whose robe is the light,
whose canopy space.
His chariots of wrath the
deep thunderclouds form,
and dark is his path on the
wings of the storm.

I PRACTICED:

☆ ☆ ☆ ☆ ☆

M	T	W	T	F	S
O	U	E	H	R	A
N	E	D	U	I	T

CYCLE 4
CONVERSION OF SAUL
WEEK 9

COLOSSIANS 1:22

But now
he has reconciled you
by Christ's physical body
through death
to present you
holy in his sight,
without blemish
and free from accusation—

related stories

Acts 9

Vos New
Testament
Lessons 64-66

Hurlbut Part 7
Lesson 6

Rho
P ρ

Sigma
Σ σ

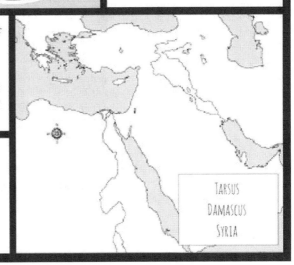

Tarsus
Damascus
Syria

BIBLE FACTS

Prophecies About Jesus
To the tune of "The Battle Hymn of the Republic," verse 3

Isaiah 40: Messenger will prepare the way,
Isaiah 61 describes His Jubilee Day,
Zechariah 11 tells the price that will be paid,
Messiah is the Way.

Refrain:
Jesus of the line of Abraham,
Jesus of the line of Isaac,
Jesus of the line of Jacob,
Born of Judah's line.

TIMELINE

Jerusalem Council

Paul's Second Journey

Thessalonians, Galatians, Romans, Corinthians

J	R	P	T	R
-5	33	46-58	70	96

hymn

O WORSHIP THE KING
verse 3

Your bountiful care,
what tongue can recite?
It breathes in the air,
it shines in the light;
it streams from the hills,
it descends to the plain,
and sweetly distills
in the dew and the rain.

I PRACTICED:

☆ ☆ ☆ ☆ ☆ ☆

M	T	W	T	F	S
O	U	E	H	R	A
N	E	D	U	I	T

CYCLE 4
PAUL'S 2nd JOURNEY
WEEK 10

COLOSSIANS 1:23a

if you continue
in your faith,
established
and firm,
not moved from the
hope held out in the
gospel.

related stories

Acts 15-18

Vos New Testament Lessons 71-80

Hurlbut Part 7 Lessons 10-14

Tau
T τ

Upsilon
Y υ

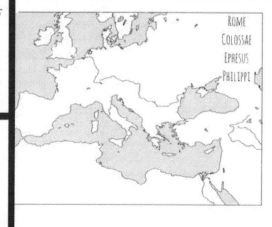

ROME
COLOSSAE
EPHESUS
PHILIPPI

BIBLE FACTS

Prophecies About Jesus
To the Tune of the "The Battle Hymn of the Republic," verse 4

Crucified with criminals: Isaiah 53,
Psalm 22: they pierced His hands and feet,
Gambling for His garments: Psalm 22, verse 18,
Messiah's work's complete!

Refrain:
Jesus of the line of Abraham,
Jesus of the line of Isaac,
Jesus of the line of Jacob,
Born of Judah's line.

TIMELINE

Paul sent to prison

Paul stands trial

Paul shipwrecked on an isle

J	R	P	T	R
-5	33	46-58	70	96

hymn

O WORSHIP THE KING
verse 4

Frail children of dust,
and feeble as frail,
in thee do we trust,
nor find thee to fail.
Thy mercies, how tender,
how firm to the end,
our Maker, Defender,
Redeemer, and Friend!

I PRACTICED:

☆ ☆ ☆ ☆ ☆ ☆

M	T	W	T	F	S
O	U	E	H	R	A
N	E	D	U	I	T

CYCLE 4
PAUL STANDS TRIAL
WEEK 11

COLOSSIANS 1:23b

This is the gospel that
you heard
and that has been
proclaimed
to every creature
under heaven,
and of which I, Paul,
have become a
servant.

related stories
Acts 22-26

Vos New
Testament
Lessons 81-87

Hurlbut Part 7
Lesson 15, 19

Phi
Φ φ

Chi
X χ

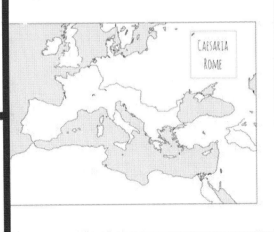

Caesaria
Rome

BIBLE FACTS

Prophecies About Jesus

To the tune of "The Battle Hymn of the Republic," verse 5

Zechariah 12: men will pierce His skin,
Isaiah 53: our sacrifice for sin,
Psalm 49: the grave cannot hold Him,
Messiah rose again!

Refrain:
Jesus of the line of Abraham,
Jesus of the line of Isaac,
Jesus of the line of Jacob,
Born of Judah's line.

TIMELINE

Paul writes more letters from prison

Titus sacks the Temple

Revelation vision

J	R	P	T	R
-5	33	46-58	70	96

hymn

O WORSHIP THE KING
verse 5

O measureless Might,
unchangeable Love,
whom angels delight
to worship above!
Thy ransomed creation,
with glory ablaze,
in true adoration
shall sing to thy praise!

I PRACTICED:

☆ ☆ ☆ ☆ ☆ ☆

M	T	W	T	F	S
O	U	E	H	R	A
N	E	D	U	I	T

CYCLE 4
TITUS SACKS THE TEMPLE
WEEK 12

COLOSSIANS 1

REVIEW!

related stories

Matthew 24
Luke 21

Psi
Ψ ψ

Omega
Ω ω

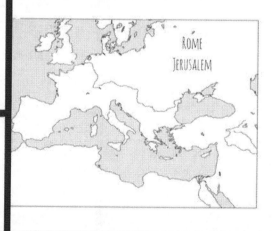
ROME
JERUSALEM

Old Testament Timeline

Creation, Fall, Cain and Abel,
Flood, Job, Tower of Babel.
Abraham, Ishmael,
Sodom and Gomorrah, Isaac as Well.

Jacob and Esau, Israel's Tribes,
Joseph in Egypt, Moses' Life.
Burning Bush and Plagues in Egypt,
Exodus and Ten Commandments.

Desert, Ark, Feasts, Tabernacle.
Joshua's Conquest, Judges Rule.
Ruth and Boaz, King Saul's Reign.
David's Kingdom, Psalms, David's
Covenant.

Solomon's Temple, Kingdom Divides,
Ahab and Elijah on the North Side,
Hezekiah and Isaiah in the South,
Israel Falls to Assyria's Clout.

Jeremiah and Ezekiel Warn Judah,
Judah Falls To Babylon.
Temple Ruined
Daniel in the Exile, Cyrus' Decree,
Exiles Return, Temple Rebuilding.

Esther Saves the Jews,
Nehemiah Builds the Wall,
Malachi Foretells John the Baptist's
Call,
Maccabean Period Ends Here,
No Word from God for 400 Years.

Old Testament Books

Genesis, Exodus, Leviticus, Numbers,
Deuteronomy, Joshua, Judges, Ruth, First
and Second Samuel, First Kings, Second
Kings, First and Second Chronicles, Ezra,
Nehemiah, Esther, Job, Psalms, Proverbs,
Ecclesiastes, Song of Solomon, Isaiah,
Jeremiah, Lamentations, Ezekiel, Daniel,
Hosea, Joel, Amos, Obadiah, Jonah, Micah,
Nahum, Habakkuk, Zephaniah, Haggai,
Zechariah, Malachi

The Judges

Othniel, Ehud, Shamgar,
Deborah, Gideon, Abimelech, Tola, Jair,
Jephthah, Ibzan, Elon, Abdon,
Samson, Eli, Samuel
Judges of Israel, Judges of Israel,
Judges of Israel,
Because God was their King.

Hymns

Be Thou My Vision
All Creatures of Our God and King
All Hail the Power of Jesus' Name

The Ten Commandments

1. I am your God;
   have no gods before Me.
2. Do not worship idols.
3. Don't take My name in vain.
4. Keep the sabbath holy.
5. Honor your father and mother.
6. Do not murder.
7. Don't commit adultery.
8. Do not steal.
9. Don't bear false witness.
10. Do not covet.

Hebrew Alphabet

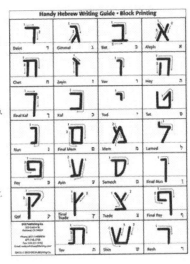

Isaiah 53

Who has believed our message
and to whom has the arm of the Lord
been revealed? He grew up before him
like a tender shoot, and like a root out of
dry ground. He had no beauty or
majesty to attract us to him, nothing in
his appearance that we should desire
him. He was despised and rejected by
men, a man of sorrows, and familiar
with suffering. Like one from
whom men hide their faces he was
despised, and we esteemed him
not. Surely he took up our infirmities
and carried our sorrows, yet we
considered him stricken by
God, smitten by him, and afflicted. But
he was pierced for our
transgressions, he was crushed for our
iniquities; the punishment that brought
us peace was upon him, and by his
wounds we are healed. We all, like
sheep, have gone astray, each of us has
turned to his own way, and the Lord
has laid on him the iniquity of us all. He
was oppressed and afflicted, yet he did
not open his mouth; he was led like a
lamb to the slaughter, and as a sheep
before her shearers is silent, so he did
not open his mouth. By oppression and
judgment he was taken away. And
who can speak of his descendants? For
he was cut off from the land of the
living; for the transgression of my
people he was stricken. He was
assigned a grave with the wicked, and
with the rich in his death, though he
had done no violence, nor was any
deceit in his mouth. Yet it was the
Lord's will to crush him and cause him
to suffer, and though the Lord makes
his life a guilt offering, he will see his
offspring and prolong his days, and the
will of the Lord will prosper in his
hand. After the suffering of his soul, he
will see the light of life and be
satisfied; by his knowledge my
righteous servant will justify many, and
he will bear their iniquities. Therefore I
will give him a portion among the
great, and he will divide the spoils with
the strong, because he poured out his
life unto death, and was numbered
with the transgressors. For he bore the
sin of many, and made intercession for
the transgressors.

New Testament Timeline

John the Baptist. Messiah Is Born.
Shepherds and Magi Visit the Lord.
Flight into Egypt. Herod's Slaughter.
Boy Jesus at the Temple.
Baptism at the Jordan.

Temptation in the Desert.
Disciples' Call. Cana Wedding.
Jubilee Inaugural
Jesus Clears the Temple.
Ministry Begins.
Meets Nicodemus and the Samaritan.

Sermon on the Mount.
Jesus Feeds 5000.
Transfiguration. Miracles Abounding.
Parables. Triumphal Entry.
Olivet Discourse on Things to Be.

Last Passover. Crucifixion.
Resurrection. Ascension.
Pentecost. Holy Spirit Received.
Peter Preaches, 3000 Believe.

Stephen Martyred. Conversion of Saul.
Paul's First Journey. Jerusalem Council.
Paul's Second Journey. Thessalonians.
Romans, Galatians, Corinthians.

Paul Sent to Prison. Paul Stands Trial.
Paul Shipwrecked on an Isle.
Paul Writes More Letters from Prison.
Titus Sacks the Temple.
Revelation Vision.

Greek Alphabet

Hymns

Blessed Assurance
When I Survey the Wondrous Cross
O Worship the King

The Fruit of the Spirit

The fruit of the Spirit is
love, joy, peace, patience,
kindness, goodness, faithfulness,
gentleness, self-control.

Prophecies About Jesus

The Bible prophesies about the coming of the Lord.
Micah 5 says Bethlehem is where He'll be born.
The virgin will give birth. Isaiah 7 has sworn
Messiah is born!

Refrain:
Jesus of the line of Abraham,
Jesus of the line of Isaac,
Jesus of the line of Jacob,
Born of Judah's line.

Second Samuel 7 says he'll sit on David's throne.
Hosea 11 says to Egypt He'll have flown.
Isaiah 7: by "Immanuel" he'll be known.
Messiah is shown. Refrain

Isaiah 40: Messenger will prepare the way.
Isaiah 61 describes His Jubilee Day.
Zechariah 11 tells the price that will be paid.
Messiah is the Way. Refrain

Crucified with criminals: Isaiah 53.
Psalm 22: they pierced His hands and feet.
Gambling for His garments: Psalm 22, verse 18
Messiah's work's complete! Refrain

Zechariah 12: men will pierce His skin.
Isaiah 53: our sacrifice for sin.
Psalm 49: the grave cannot hold Him,
Messiah rose again! Refrain

Colossians 1:15-23

He is the image of the invisible
God, the firstborn over all creation.
For by him all things were created:
things in heaven and on earth,
visible and invisible, whether
thrones or powers or rulers or
authorities; all things were created
by him and for him. He is before all
things, and in him all things hold
together. And he is the head of the
body, the church; he is the
beginning and the firstborn from
among the dead, so that in
everything he might have the
supremacy. For God was pleased
to have all his fullness dwell in
him, and through him to reconcile
to himself all things, whether
things on earth or things in
heaven, by making peace through
his blood, shed on the cross.

Once you were alienated from
God and were enemies in your
minds because of your evil
behavior. But now he has
reconciled you by Christ's physical
body through death to present
you holy in his sight, without
blemish and free from accusation
— if you continue in your faith,
established and firm, not moved
from the hope held out in the
gospel. This is the gospel that you
heard and that has been
proclaimed to every creature
under heaven, and of which I, Paul,
have become a servant.

New Testament Books

Matthew, Mark, Luke and John,
Acts and the letter to the Romans,
First and Second Corinthians,
Galatians and Ephesians,
Philippians, Colossians,
First and Second Thessalonians,
First and Second Timothy,
Titus and Philemon,
Hebrews and the book of James,
First and Second Peter,
First and Second, Third John,
Jude and Revelation

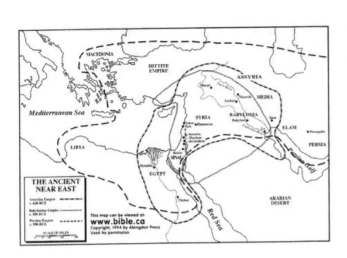

THE ANCIENT
NEAR EAST

Israel
at the
Time of Christ
30 AD

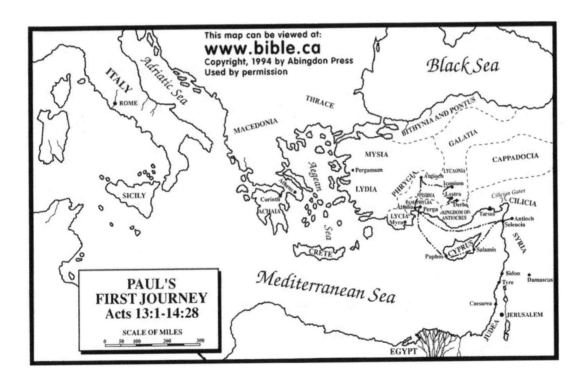

PAUL'S
FIRST JOURNEY
Acts 13:1-14:28

SCALE OF MILES

Classical
Sunday School

FAMILY DRILL BOOK

CYCLES 5 & 6

To learn more about Classical education, and for
great tips on using this Drill Book, go to
StrongHappyFamily.org

BIBLE FACTS

Plagues in Egypt

- Water (to blood)
- Frogs
- Gnats
- Flies
- Cattle
- Boils
- Hail
- Locusts
- Darkness
- Death (of the firstborn)

- We
- Find
- God
- Forgives
- Children
- But
- Hates
- Lousy
- Dirty
- Deeds

TIMELINE

Creation

Fall

Cain and Abel

hymn

JESUS PAID IT ALL
verse 1

I hear the Savior say,
"Thy strength indeed is small,
Child of weakness, watch
and pray,
Find in Me thine all in all."

REFRAIN:
Jesus paid it all,
All to Him I owe;
Sin had left a crimson stain,
He washed it white as snow.

I PRACTICED:

☆ ☆ ☆ ☆ ☆ ☆
M T W T F S
O U E H R A
N E D U I T

CYCLE 5
CAIN AND ABEL
WEEK 1

EXODUS 20:2-3

I am the Lord your
God, who brought
you out of Egypt, out
of the land of slavery.

You shall have no
other gods before Me.

related stories

Genesis 4

Vos Old
Testament
Lessons 8-9

Hurlbut Part 1
Lesson 2

Hear
שְׁמַע
Shema

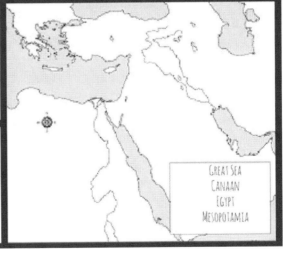

Great Sea
Canaan
Egypt
Mesopotamia

BIBLE FACTS

Plagues in Egypt

- Water (to blood)
- Frogs
- Gnats
- Flies
- Cattle
- Boils
- Hail
- Locusts
- Darkness
- Death (of the firstborn)

- We
- Find
- God
- Forgives
- Children
- But
- Hates
- Lousy
- Dirty
- Deeds

TIMELINE

Flood

Job

Tower of Babel

hymn

JESUS PAID IT ALL
verse 2

Lord, now indeed I find
Thy pow'r and Thine alone,
Can change the leper's spots
And melt the heart of stone.

REFRAIN:
Jesus paid it all,
All to Him I owe;
Sin had left a crimson stain,
He washed it white as snow.

I PRACTICED:

☆ ☆ ☆ ☆ ☆ ☆

M	T	W	T	F	S
O	U	E	H	R	A
N	E	D	U	I	T

CYCLE 5
TOWER OF BABEL
WEEK 2

EXODUS 20:4

You shall not make for yourself an image in the form of anything in heaven above or on the earth beneath or in the waters below.

related stories

Genesis 11

Vos Old Testament Lesson 11

Hurlbut Part 1 Lesson 4

O Israel

יִשְׂרָאֵל

Yisrael

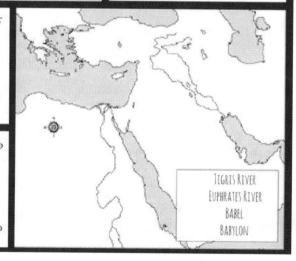

TIGRIS RIVER
EUPHRATES RIVER
BABEL
BABYLON

BIBLE FACTS

Plagues in Egypt

- Water (to blood)
- Frogs
- Gnats
- Flies
- Cattle
- Boils
- Hail
- Locusts
- Darkness
- Death (of the firstborn)

- We
- Find
- God
- Forgives
- Children
- But
- Hates
- Lousy
- Dirty
- Deeds

TIMELINE

Abraham

Ishmael

Sodom and Gomorrah

A	M	D	E
2000	1500	1000	500

hymn

JESUS PAID IT ALL
verse 3

For nothing good have I
Where-by Thy grace to claim;
I'll wash my garments white
In the blood of Calv'ry's Lamb.

REFRAIN:
Jesus paid it all,
All to Him I owe;
Sin had left a crimson stain,
He washed it white as snow.

I PRACTICED:

☆ ☆ ☆ ☆ ☆ ☆

M	T	W	T	F	S
O	U	E	H	R	A
N	E	D	U	I	T

CYCLE 5
SODOM AND GOMORRAH
WEEK 3

EXODUS 20:5

You shall not bow down to them or worship them; for I, the Lord your God, am a jealous God, punishing the children for the sin of the parents to the third and fourth generation of those who hate Me.

related stories

Genesis 18-19

Vos Old Testament Lesson 14

Hurlbut Part 1 Lesson 6-8

Yahweh
יהוה
Yahweh

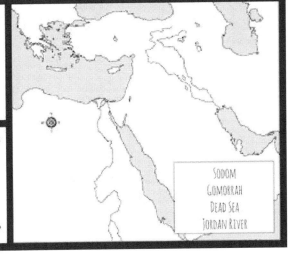

Sodom
Gomorrah
Dead Sea
Jordan River

BIBLE FACTS

Plagues in Egypt

- Water (to blood)
- Frogs
- Gnats
- Flies
- Cattle
- Boils
- Hail
- Locusts
- Darkness
- Death (of the firstborn)

- We
- Find
- God
- Forgives
- Children
- But
- Hates
- Lousy
- Dirty
- Deeds

TIMELINE

Isaac as well

Jacob and Esau

Israel's tribes

A	M	D	E
2000	1500	1000	500

hymn

JESUS PAID IT ALL
verse 4

And when, before the throne,
I stand in Him complete,
"Jesus died my soul to save,"
My lips shall still repeat.

REFRAIN:
Jesus paid it all,
All to Him I owe;
Sin had left a crimson stain,
He washed it white as snow.

I PRACTICED:

☆ ☆ ☆ ☆ ☆

M	T	W	T	F	S
O	U	E	H	R	A
N	E	D	U	I	T

CYCLE 5
ISRAEL'S TRIBES
WEEK 4

EXODUS 20:6

but showing love to a thousand generations of those who love Me and keep My commandments.

related stories

Genesis 35

Vos Old Testament Lessons 18-23

Hurlbut Part 1 Lessons 13

our God
אֱלֹהֵינוּ
eloheynu

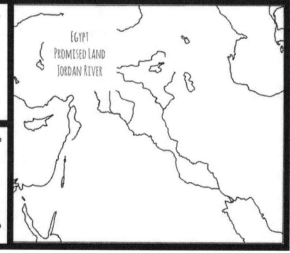

EGYPT
PROMISED LAND
JORDAN RIVER

BIBLE FACTS

The Feasts of the Lord

A RHYTHMIC CHANT

Passover: Saved by the blood of the lamb,
Unleavened Bread: Dead to sin, I am
Firstfruits: Celebrates life from the ground
Pentecost: Making laws and vows
Rosh Hashanah: New Year trumpets play
Yom Kippur: Atonement day
Tabernacles: Joy and peace
These are God's Appointed Feasts

TIMELINE

Joseph in Egypt

Moses' Life

Burning bush and plagues in Egypt

_A____M____D____E_
2000   1500   1000   500

hymn

A MIGHTY FORTRESS
verse 1

A mighty fortress is our God,
a bulwark never failing;
our helper He, amid the flood
of mortal ills prevailing.
For still our ancient foe
does seek to work us woe;
his craft and power are great,
and armed with cruel hate,
on earth is not his equal.

I PRACTICED:

☆ ☆ ☆ ☆ ☆ ☆
M T W T F S
O U E H R A
N E D U I T

CYCLE 5
BURNING BUSH
PLAGUES IN EGYPT
WEEK 5

EXODUS 20:7

You shall not misuse the name of the Lord your God, for the Lord will not hold anyone guiltless who misuses His name.

related stories

Exodus 3-12

Vos Old Testament Lessons 33-34

Hurlbut Part 1 Lessons 21-23

Yahweh
יהוה
Yahweh

MIDIAN
MOUNT HOREB
PROMISED LAND
EGYPT

BIBLE FACTS
The Feasts of the Lord
A RHYTHMIC CHANT

Passover: Saved by the blood of the lamb,

Unleavened Bread: Dead to sin, I am

Firstfruits: Celebrates life from the ground

Pentecost: Making laws and vows

Rosh Hashanah: New Year trumpets play

Yom Kippur: Atonement day

Tabernacles: Joy and peace

These are God's Appointed Feasts

TIMELINE

Exodus and 10 Commandments

Desert, Ark, Feasts, Tabernacle

Joshua's Conquest

_A_	_M_	_D_	_E_
2000	1500	1000	500

hymn

A MIGHTY FORTRESS
verse 2

Did we in our own strength confide,
our striving would be losing,
were not the right Man on our side,
the Man of God's own choosing.
You ask who that may be?
Christ Jesus, it is He;
Lord Sabaoth His name,
from age to age the same;
and He must win the battle.

I PRACTICED:

☆ ☆ ☆ ☆ ☆ ☆

M	T	W	T	F	S
O	U	E	H	R	A
N	E	D	U	I	T

CYCLE 5
JOSHUA'S CONQUEST
WEEK 6

EXODUS 20:8

Remember the Sabbath day by keeping it holy.

related stories

Joshua 1-24

Vos Old Testament Lessons 53-56

Hurlbut Part 2 Lessons 1-5

(is) one

אֶחָד

echad

REUBEN
SIMEON
JUDAH
ISSACHAR
ZEBULUN
EPHRAIM
MANNASEH
BENJAMIN
NAPHTALI
DAN
GAD
ASHER

BIBLE FACTS

The Feasts of the Lord

A RHYTHMIC CHANT

Passover: Saved by the blood of the lamb,

Unleavened Bread: Dead to sin, I am

Firstfruits: Celebrates life from the ground

Pentecost: Making laws and vows

Rosh Hashanah: New Year trumpets play

Yom Kippur: Atonement day

Tabernacles: Joy and peace

These are God's Appointed Feasts

TIMELINE

Judges rule

Ruth and Boaz

King Saul's reign

A	M	D	E
2000	1500	1000	500

hymn

A MIGHTY FORTRESS
verse 3

And though this world,
with devils filled,
should threaten to undo us,
we will not fear,
for God has willed
His truth to triumph through us.
The prince of darkness grim,
we tremble not for him;
his rage we can endure,
for lo! his doom is sure;
one little word shall fell him.

I PRACTICED:

☆ ☆ ☆ ☆ ☆ ☆

M	T	W	T	F	S
O	U	E	H	R	A
N	E	D	U	I	T

CYCLE 5

KING SAUL'S REIGN

WEEK 7

EXODUS 20:9

Six days you
shall labor
and do all
your work,

related stories
1 Samuel 8-31

Vos Old
Testament
Lessons 65-71

Hurlbut Part 2
Lesson 18
Part 3 Lessons 1-9

Hear, O Israel,
Yahweh, our
Yahweh (is) one.
שְׁמַע יִשְׂרָאֵל יהוה
אֱלֹהֵינוּ יהוה אֶחָד
Shema Yisrael
Yahweh eloheynu
Yahweh echad

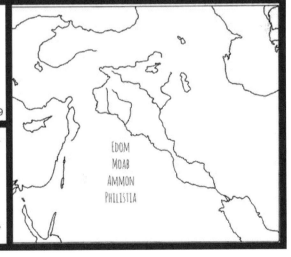

EDOM
MOAB
AMMON
PHILISTIA

BIBLE FACTS

The Feasts of the Lord

A RHYTHMIC CHANT

Passover: Saved by the blood of the lamb,

Unleavened Bread: Dead to sin, I am

Firstfruits: Celebrates life from the ground

Pentecost: Making laws and vows

Rosh Hashanah: New Year trumpets play

Yom Kippur: Atonement day

Tabernacles: Joy and peace

These are God's Appointed Feasts

TIMELINE

David's Kingdom

Psalms, Covenant

Solomon's Temple, Kingdom divides

A	M	D	E
2000	1500	1000	500

hymn

A MIGHTY FORTRESS
verse 4

That Word above all earthly powers
no thanks to them abideth;
the Spirit and the gifts are ours
through Him who with us sideth.
Let goods and kindred go.
this mortal life also;
the body they may kill:
God's truth abideth still;
His kingdom is forever!

I PRACTICED:

☆ ☆ ☆ ☆ ☆ ☆

M	T	W	T	F	S
O	U	E	H	R	A
N	E	D	U	I	T

CYCLE 5
SOLOMON'S TEMPLE
KINGDOM DIVIDES
WEEK 8

EXODUS 20:10

but the seventh day is a sabbath to the Lord your God. On it you shall not do any work, neither you, nor your son or daughter, nor your male or female servant, nor your animals, nor any foreigner residing in your towns.

related stories

1 Kings 2-13

Vos Old Testament Lessons 76-79

Hurlbut Part 3 Lessons 17-20, Part 4 Lesson 1

Blessed
בָּרוּךְ
Barukh

Jerusalem
Lebanon
Sheba

BIBLE FACTS

COVENANTS, V. 1

TO THE TUNE OF "THE OLD GREY MARE"

God made many promises

called covenants,

The first, the Adamic, says

a Savior will be sent,

Noahic says there won't

again be sent,

A flood to destroy the earth.

TIMELINE

Ahab and Elijah on the north side

Hezekiah and Isaiah in the South

Israel falls to Assyria's clout

A	M	D	E
2000	1500	1000	500

hymn

CROWN HIM WITH MANY CROWNS
verse 1

Crown Him with many crowns,
The Lamb upon His throne;
Hark! How the
heav'nly anthem drowns
All music but its own!
Awake, my soul and sing
Of Him Who died for thee,
And hail Him
as thy matchless King
Through all eternity.

I PRACTICED:

☆ ☆ ☆ ☆ ☆

M	T	W	T	F	S
O	U	E	H	R	A
N	E	D	U	I	T

CYCLE 5
ISRAEL FALLS TO ASSYRIA
WEEK 9

EXODUS 20:11

For in six days the Lord made the heavens and the earth, the sea, and all that is in them, but He rested on the seventh day. Therefore the Lord blessed the Sabbath day and made it holy.

related stories

2 Kings 15

Vos Old Testament Lesson 94

Hurlbut Part 4 Lessons 17-18

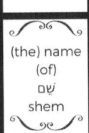

(the) name (of)
שֵׁם
shem

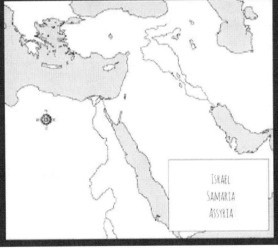

ISRAEL
SAMARIA
ASSYRIA

BIBLE FACTS

Covenants, V. 2

To the tune of "The Old Grey Mare"

Abrahamic Covenant pledged

at God's command:

A great name, a nation,

and a promised land,

Descendants just as numerous

as sand,

A blessing to all the earth.

TIMELINE

Jeremiah and Ezekiel
warn Judah

Judah falls to Babylon,
Temple ruined

Daniel in the Exile

_A___ _M___ _D___E__
2000   1500   1000   500

hymn

CROWN HIM WITH MANY CROWNS
verse 2

Crown Him the Lord of love!
Behold His hands and side—
Rich wounds,
yet visible above.
In beauty glorified.
No angel in the sky
Can fully bear that sight,
But downward bends his
wond'ring eye
At mysteries so bright.

I PRACTICED:

☆ ☆ ☆ ☆ ☆ ☆

M	T	W	T	F	S
O	U	E	H	R	A
N	E	D	U	I	T

CYCLE 5

DANIEL IN THE EXILE

WEEK 10

EXODUS 20:12

Honor your father
and your mother,
so that you may
live long in the
land the Lord your
God is giving you.

related stories

Daniel 1-12

Vos Old
Testament
Lessons 100-104

Hurlbut Part 5
Lessons 8-12

glorious
kingdom
כְּבוֹד מַלְכוּתוֹ
kevod
malkuto

BABYLON
PERSIA
GREECE
ROME

BIBLE FACTS

Covenants, v. 3

To the tune of "The Old Grey Mare"

Mosaic says obey the law

and you'll be fine,

Davidic: eternal king

from David's line,

New Covenant: I will make

this people mine

God's promise to all the earth!

TIMELINE

Cyrus' decree
Exiles return

Temple rebuilding

Esther saves the
Jews

_A_____M_____D_____E__
2000   1500   1000   500

hymn

CROWN HIM
WITH MANY CROWNS
verse 3

Crown Him the Lord of life!
Who triumphed o'er the grave,
Who rose victorious in the strife
For those He came to save.
His glories now we sing,
Who died, and rose on high,
Who died eternal life to bring,
And lives that death may die.

I PRACTICED:

☆ ☆ ☆ ☆ ☆ ☆
M T W T F S
O U E H R A
N E D U I T

CYCLE 5
ESTHER SAVES THE JEWS
WEEK 11

EXODUS 20:13–16

You shall not murder.

You shall not commit adultery.

You shall not steal.

You shall not give false testimony against your neighbor.

related stories

Esther 1-10

Vos Old Testament Lessons 107-108

Hurlbut Part 5 Lesson 15

forever and ever

לְעוֹלָם וָעֶד

l'olam va-ed

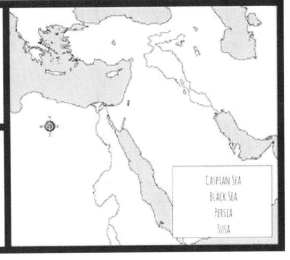

CASPIAN SEA
BLACK SEA
PERSIA
SUSA

BIBLE FACTS
Covenants
To the tune of "The Old Grey Mare"

God made many promises called covenants.
The first, the Adamic, says a Savior will be sent.
Noahic says there won't again be sent
A flood to destroy the earth.

Abrahamic Covenant pledged at God's command:
A great name, a nation, and a promised land,
Descendants just as numerous as sand,
A blessing to all the earth.

Mosaic says obey the law and you'll be fine.
Davidic: eternal king from David's line.
New Covenant: I will make this people mine.
God's promise to all the earth

TIMELINE

Nehemiah builds the wall

Malachi foretells John the Baptist's call

Maccabean period ends here, no word from God for 400 years

_A_____	___M___	___D___	___E__
2000	1500	1000	500

hymn

CROWN HIM WITH MANY CROWNS
verse 4

Crown Him the Lord of heav'n!
One with the Father known,
One with the Spirit
through Him giv'n
From yonder glorious throne.
To Thee be endless praise.
For Thou for us hast died;
Be Thou, O Lord,
through endless days
Adored and magnified.

I PRACTICED:

☆ ☆ ☆ ☆ ☆ ☆

M	T	W	T	F	S
O	U	E	H	R	A
N	E	D	U	I	T

CYCLE 5
MACCABEAN PERIOD
WEEK 12

EXODUS 20:2-17

REVIEW!

related stories

Hurlbut Part 5
Lesson 16

Blessed be the name
of His glorious
kingdom forever
and ever.
בָּרוּךְ שֵׁם כְּבוֹד מַלְכוּתוֹ
לְעוֹלָם וָעֶד
Barukh shem kevod
malkuto l'olam
va-ed.

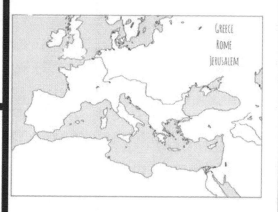

GREECE
ROME
JERUSALEM

BIBLE FACTS
Paul's Journeys

"Go! Let's Go" used by permission from David Heath-Whyte
©2004 Maynard's Groovy Bible Tunes

Go! Let's go 'round the Mediterranean,
Go! Let's go with the Gospel and Paul,
Go! Let's go all around the world,
Telling everybody that Jesus is Lord.

On the road to Damascus,
Paul met Jesus alive!
Never would be the same again,
Once the scales had cleared from his eyes.

TIMELINE

John the Baptist

Messiah is born

Shepherds and
Magi visit the Lord

J	R	P	T	R
-5	33	46-58	70	96

hymn
COME, THOU FOUNT
verse 1

Come, thou Fount of every blessing,
tune my heart to sing Thy grace;
streams of mercy, never ceasing,
call for songs of loudest praise.
Teach me some melodious sonnet,
sung by flaming tongues above.
Praise the mount I'm fixed upon it
mount of God's redeeming love.

I PRACTICED:

☆ ☆ ☆ ☆ ☆ ☆

M	T	W	T	F	S
O	U	E	H	R	A
N	E	D	U	I	T

CYCLE 6
SHEPHERDS AND MAGI
WEEK 1

Philippians 2:1

If you have any
encouragement from
being united with
Christ, if any comfort
from His love, if any
fellowship with the
Spirit, if any tenderness
and compassion,

related stories
Matthew 2
Luke 2

Vos New
Testament
Lesson 4

Hurlbut Part 6
Lessons 2-3

(the) God

ὁ θεός

(o) theós

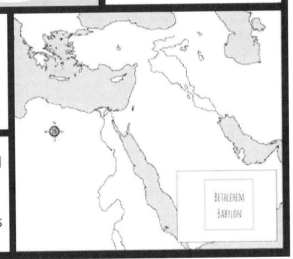

Bethlehem
Babylon

BIBLE FACTS

PAUL'S JOURNEYS

"Go! Let's Go" used by permission from David Heath-Whyte
©2004 Maynard's Groovy Bible Tunes

Go! Let's go 'round the Mediterranean,

Go! Let's go with the Gospel and Paul,

Go! Let's go all around the world,

Telling everybody that Jesus is Lord.

Paul and Silas in prison,

Chained up to a wall,

Singing out their hearts with joy,

Knowing Jesus was in control.

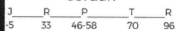

TIMELINE

Flight into Egypt
Herod's Slaughter

Boy Jesus at the Temple

Baptism at the Jordan

J	R	P	T	R
-5	33	46-58	70	96

hymn

COME THOU FOUNT
verse 2

Here I raise my Ebenezer;
hither by Thy help I've come;
and I hope, by thy good pleasure,
safely to arrive at home.
Jesus sought me when a stranger,
wandering from the fold of God;
He, to rescue me from danger,
interposed His precious blood.

I PRACTICED:

☆ ☆ ☆ ☆ ☆ ☆

M	T	W	T	F	S
O	U	E	H	R	A
N	E	D	U	I	T

CYCLE 6
BAPTISM AT JORDAN
WEEK 2

Philippians 2:2

then make my joy
complete by being
like-minded, having
the same love,
being one in spirit
and purpose.

related stories

Matthew 3

Vos New Testament Lesson 7

Hurlbut Part 6 Lesson 6

is
εἴναι
eínai
(EE-ne)

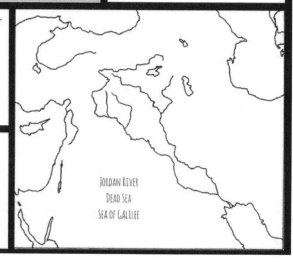

Jordan River
Dead Sea
Sea of Galilee

BIBLE FACTS

Paul's Journeys

"GO! LET'S GO" USED BY PERMISSION FROM DAVID HEATH-WHYTE
©2004 MAYNARD'S GROOVY BIBLE TUNES

Go! Let's go 'round the Mediterranean,
Go! Let's go with the Gospel and Paul,
Go! Let's go all around the world,
Telling everybody that Jesus is Lord.

Started out from Antioch,
Spreading Jesus' word,
Four long journeys later, he's in Rome
And thousands of people have heard!

TIMELINE

Temptation in the desert

Disciples' Call

Cana Wedding
Jubilee Inaugural

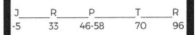

J	R	P	T	R
-5	33	46-58	70	96

hymn

COME THOU FOUNT
verse 3

Oh, to grace how great a debtor
daily I'm constrained to be!
Let Thy goodness, like a fetter,
bind my wandering heart to Thee:
prone to wander, Lord, I feel it,
prone to leave the God I love;
here's my heart, O take and seal it;
seal it for Thy courts above.

I PRACTICED:

☆ ☆ ☆ ☆ ☆
M	T	W	T	F	S
O	U	E	H	R	A
N	E	D	U	I	T

CYCLE 6
CANA WEDDING
JUBILEE INAUGURAL
WEEK 3

Philippians 2:3

Do nothing out of selfish ambition or vain conceit, but in humility consider others better than yourselves.

related stories

Luke 4
John 2

Vos New Testament
Lesson 10

Hurlbut Part 6
Lessons 7, 9

love
αγάπη
agápi

CANA
CAPERNAUM
NAZARETH

BIBLE FACTS

Paul's Journeys

"Go! Let's Go" used by permission from David Heath-Whyte
©2004 Maynard's Groovy Bible Tunes

Go! Let's go 'round the Mediterranean,
Go! Let's go with the Gospel and Paul,
Go! Let's go all around the world,
Telling everybody that Jesus is Lord.

Shipwrecked, beaten, stoned and more
-always carrying on.
Sharing Jesus everywhere-
Knowing He's for everyone!

TIMELINE

Jesus clears the Temple, Ministry begins

Meets Nicodemus and the Samaritan

Sermon on the Mount

J	R	P	T	R
-5	33	46-58	70	96

hymn

HOW FIRM A FOUNDATION
verse 1

How firm a foundation
you saints of the Lord,
is laid for your faith
in His excellent Word!
What more can He say
than to you He has said,
to you who for refuge
to Jesus have fled?

I PRACTICED:

☆ ☆ ☆ ☆ ☆ ☆

M	T	W	T	F	S
O	U	E	H	R	A
N	E	D	U	I	T

CYCLE 6
Sermon on the Mount
WEEK 4

Philippians 2:4

Each of you should look not only to your own interests, but also to the interests of others.

related stories

Matthew 5-7

Vos New Testament Lesson 20

Hurlbut Part 6 Lesson 13

God is love.

Ο Θεός είναι αγάπη.

O Theós eínai agápi.

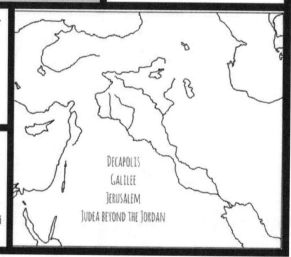

Decapolis
Galilee
Jerusalem
Judea beyond the Jordan

BIBLE FACTS
Jesus' Sayings on the Cross
To the tune of "Hark the Herald Angels Sing"

- Father, forgive them, for they know not what they do.
- I tell you the truth today, you'll be with Me in paradise.
- Woman, here's your son; here is your mother.
- My God, My god, why have You forsaken Me?
- I thirst.
- It is finished.
- Father, into Your hands I commit My spirit.

TIMELINE

Jesus feeds 5000,

Transfiguration,

Miracles abounding

J	R	P	T	R
-5	33	46-58	70	96

hymn

HOW FIRM A FOUNDATION
verse 2

"Fear not, I am with you,
O be not dismayed,
for I am your God,
and will still give you aid;
I'll strengthen you,
help you,
and cause you to stand,
upheld by My righteous,
omnipotent hand."

I PRACTICED:

☆ ☆ ☆ ☆ ☆ ☆

M	T	W	T	F	S
O	U	E	H	R	A
N	E	D	U	I	T

CYCLE 6
MIRACLES
WEEK 5

Your attitude
should be the
same as that of
Christ Jesus:

related stories
Mark 1

Vos New
Testament
Lessons 14-7, 19,
21, 23-4, 27-9, 38

Hurlbut Part 6
Lesson 14, 16-7,
24, 26

In (the)
beginning

Ἐν ἀρχῇ

En ar-KAY

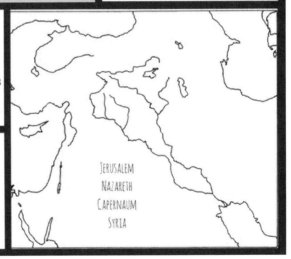

Jerusalem
Nazareth
Capernaum
Syria

BIBLE FACTS

Jesus' Sayings on the Cross
To the tune of "Hark the Herald Angels Sing"

- Father, forgive them, for they know not what they do.
- I tell you the truth today, you'll be with Me in paradise.
- Woman, here's your son; here is your mother.
- My God, My god, why have You forsaken Me?
- I thirst.
- It is finished.
- Father, into Your hands I commit My spirit.

TIMELINE

Parables

Triumphal Entry

Olivet Discourse on things to be

J	R	P	T	R
-5	33	46-58	70	96

hymn

HOW FIRM A FOUNDATION
verse 3

"When through the deep waters
I call you to go,
the rivers of sorrow
shall not overflow,
for I will be with you
in trouble to bless,
and sanctify to you
your deepest distress."

I PRACTICED:

☆ ☆ ☆ ☆ ☆ ☆

M	T	W	T	F	S
O	U	E	H	R	A
N	E	D	U	I	T

CYCLE 6
OLIVET DISCOURSE
WEEK 6

Philippians 2:6

Who, being in very nature God, did not consider equality with God something to be grasped,

related stories

Matthew 24-25

Vos New Testament Lesson 43

Hurlbut Part 6 Lesson 32

was the Word

ἦν ὁ λόγος

ayn ha LOH-gohs

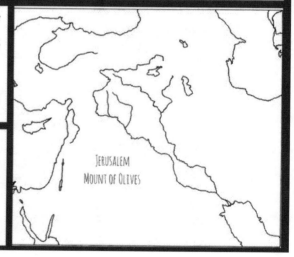

Jerusalem
Mount of Olives

BIBLE FACTS

Jesus' Sayings on the Cross
To the tune of "Hark the Herald Angels Sing"

- Father, forgive them, for they know not what they do.
- I tell you the truth today, you'll be with Me in paradise.
- Woman, here's your son; here is your mother.
- My God, My god, why have You forsaken Me?
- I thirst.
- It is finished.
- Father, into Your hands I commit My spirit.

TIMELINE

Last Passover

Crucifixion

Resurrection

J	R	P	T	R
-5	33	46-58	70	96

hymn

HOW FIRM A FOUNDATION
verse 4

"When through fiery trials
your pathway shall lie,
My grace all-sufficient
shall be your supply;
the flame shall not hurt you;
I only design
your dross to consume
and your gold to refine."

I PRACTICED:

☆ ☆ ☆ ☆ ☆ ☆
M T W T F S
O U E H R A
N E D U I T

CYCLE 6
RESURRECTION
WEEK 7

Philippians 2:7

but made Himself nothing,

taking the very nature of a servant,

being made in human likeness.

related stories
Luke 24 John 20

Vos New
Testament
Lessons 52-54

Hurlbut Part 6
Lesson 37

and the Word

καὶ ὁ λόγος

kī ha
LOH-gohs

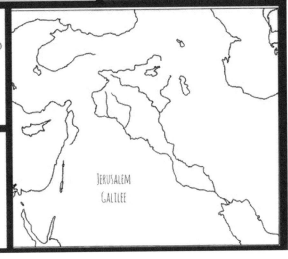

JERUSALEM
GALILEE

BIBLE FACTS

Jesus' Sayings on the Cross

To the tune of "Hark the Herald Angels Sing"

- Father, forgive them, for they know not what they do.

- I tell you the truth today, you'll be with Me in paradise.

- Woman, here's your son; here is your mother.

- My God, My god, why have You forsaken Me?

- I thirst.

- It is finished.

- Father, into Your hands I commit My spirit.

TIMELINE

Ascension

Pentecost, Holy Spirit received

Peter preaches, 3,000 believe

J	R	P	T	R
-5	33	46-58	70	96

hymn

HOW FIRM A FOUNDATION
verse 5

"The soul that on Jesus
has leaned for repose
I will not, I will not
desert to its foes;
that soul, though all hell
should endeavor to shake,
I'll never, no, never,
no never forsake!"

I PRACTICED:

☆ ☆ ☆ ☆ ☆ ☆

M	T	W	T	F	S
O	U	E	H	R	A
N	E	D	U	I	T

CYCLE 6
PETER PREACHES
3,000 BELIEVE
WEEK 8

Philippians 2:8

And being found in appearance as a man, He humbled Himself and became obedient to death-- even death on a cross!

related stories
Acts 2

Vos New Testament Lessons 57-60, 62, 67, 70

Hurlbut Part 7 Lessons 2, 3, 5, 7, 8

was with the God

ἦν πρὸς τὸν θεόν

ayn pros ton theos

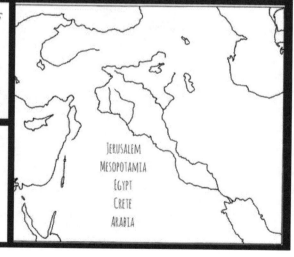

Jerusalem
Mesopotamia
Egypt
Crete
Arabia

BIBLE FACTS
REVIEW!

NAMES OF JESUS

Alpha, Omega, Lion of Judah,
Messiah, Shepherd of the Sheep,
Immanuel, Friend, Lord of Glory,
Our Passover, Our Great High Priest.

Prophet, Lord, Savior, and King of all Kings,
Mediator 'tween God and Men,
Rock, Vine, Bread of Life, and the Good Shepherd,
The Firstborn from the Dead.

Only Begotten of the Father,
Rabbi, the Seed of Abraham,
The Last Adam, the Word Become Flesh,
Son of God, the Son of Man.

The Lord of all Lords, God's Pascal Lamb,
Morning Star and Chief Cornerstone,
Light of the World, Bread Come Down from Heaven,
Redeemer, Master, God's Holy One

Head of the Whole Church and Heir of All Things,
The Captain of our Salvation,
Author and Finisher of our Faith, Door,
The Desire of Nations.

TWELVE DISCIPLES

Peter, Andrew,
James and John,
Fishermen of
Capernaum,
Thomas and
Saint Matthew too,
Philip and
Bartholomew,
James, his brother
Thaddeus,
Simon and the one
called Judas,
Twelve Disciples,
Jesus chose,
Called Apostles
when He rose.

TIMELINE

Stephen martyred

Conversion of Saul

Paul's first journey

J	R	P	T	R
-5	33	46-58	70	96

hymn

COME, YE THANKFUL PEOPLE, COME
verse 1

Come, ye thankful people, come,
raise the song of harvest home;
all is safely gathered in,
ere the winter storms begin.
God our Maker doth provide
for our wants to be supplied;
come to God's own temple, come,
raise the song of harvest home.

I PRACTICED:

☆ ☆ ☆ ☆ ☆

M	T	W	T	F	S
O	U	E	H	R	A
N	E	D	U	I	T

CYCLE 6
PAUL'S FIRST JOURNEY
WEEK 9

Philippians 2:9

Therefore God
exalted Him to the
highest place

and gave Him the
name that is above
every name,

related stories

Acts 13-14

Vos New
Testament
Lessons 71-72

Hurlbut Part 7
Lesson 9

and God

καὶ θεὸς

kī theos

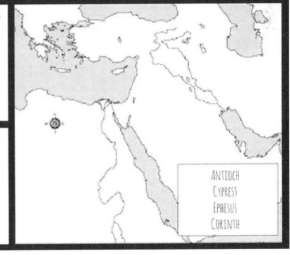

ANTIOCH
CYPRESS
EPHESUS
CORINTH

BIBLE FACTS
REVIEW!

The Apostles' Creed

I believe in God, the Father Almighty,
Maker of heaven and earth; And in Jesus
Christ, His only begotten Son, our Lord;
Who was conceived by the Holy Spirit,
Born of the Virgin Mary, Suffered under
Pontius Pilate, Was crucified, dead and
buried; He descended into hell; The
third day He rose again from the dead;
He ascended into Heaven, And sitteth
at the right hand of God the Father
Almighty; From thence He shall come
to judge the living and the dead. I
believe in the Holy Spirit; the holy
catholic Church, the communion of
saints, the forgiveness of sins; The
resurrection of the body, and life
everlasting. Amen.

New Testament Books

Matthew, Mark, Luke and John,
Acts and the letter to the Romans,
First and Second Corinthians,
Galatians and Ephesians,
Philippians, Colossians,
First and Second Thessalonians,
First and Second Timothy,
Titus and Philemon,
Hebrews and the book of James,
First and Second Peter,
First and Second, Third John,
Jude and Revelation

TIMELINE

Jerusalem Council

Paul's Second Journey

Thessalonians, Galatians, Romans, Corinthians

J	R	P	T	R
-5	33	46-58	70	96

hymn

COME, YE THANKFUL PEOPLE, COME
verse 2

All the world is God's own field,
fruit as praise to God we yield;
wheat and tares together sown
are to joy or sorrow grown;
first the blade and then the ear,
then the full corn shall appear;
Lord of harvest, grant that we
wholesome grain and pure may b

I PRACTICED:

☆ ☆ ☆ ☆ ☆ ☆

M	T	W	T	F	S
O	U	E	H	R	A
N	E	D	U	I	T

CYCLE 6
THESSALONIANS, GALATIANS, ROMANS, CORINTHIANS
WEEK 10

Philippians 2:10

that at the name
of Jesus

every knee
should bow,

in heaven
and on earth
and under the earth.

related stories

Thessalonians,
Galatians,
Romans,
Corinthians

Hurlbut Part 7
Lesson 13

was the
Word

ἦν ὁ λόγος

nee logos

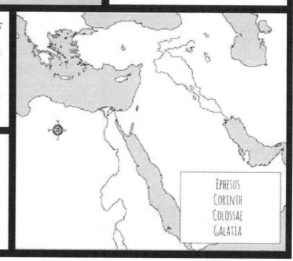

EPHESUS
CORINTH
COLOSSAE
GALATIA

BIBLE FACTS
REVIEW!

Old Testament Prophecies About Jesus

The Bible prophesies about the coming of the Lord.
Micah 5 says Bethlehem is where He'll be born.
The virgin will give birth. Isaiah 7 has sworn
Messiah is born!

Refrain:
Jesus of the line of Abraham,
Jesus of the line of Isaac,
Jesus of the line of Jacob.
Born of Judah's line.

Second Samuel 7 says he'll sit on David's throne.
Hosea 11 says to Egypt He'll have flown.
Isaiah 7: by "Immanuel" he'll be known.
Messiah is shown. Refrain

Isaiah 40: Messenger will prepare the way.
Isaiah 61 describes His Jubilee Day.
Zechariah 11 tells the price that will be paid.
Messiah is the Way. Refrain

Crucified with criminals: Isaiah 53.
Psalm 22: they pierced His hands and feet.
Gambling for His garments: Psalm 22, verse 18.
Messiah's work's complete! Refrain

Zechariah 12: men will pierce His skin.
Isaiah 53: our sacrifice for sin.
Psalm 49: the grave cannot hold Him.
Messiah rose again! Refrain

The Fruit of the Spirit

- love
- joy
- peace
- patience
- kindness
- goodness
- faithfulness
- gentleness
- self-control

TIMELINE

Paul sent to prison

Paul stands trial

Paul shipwrecked on an isle

J	R	P	T	R
-5	33	46-58	70	96

hymn

COME, YE THANKFUL PEOPLE, COME
verse 3

For the Lord our God shall come.

and shall take the harvest home;

from the field shall in that day

all offenses purge away.

giving angels charge at last

in the fire the tares to cast;

but the fruitful ears to store

in the garner evermore.

I PRACTICED:

☆ ☆ ☆ ☆ ☆ ☆

M	T	W	T	F	S
O	U	E	H	R	A
N	E	D	U	I	T

CYCLE 6
PAUL SHIPWRECKED
WEEK 11

Philippians 2:11

and every tongue confess

that Jesus Christ is Lord,

to the glory of God the Father.

related stories

Acts 27-28

Vos New Testament Lessons 88-91

Hurlbut Part 7 Lesson 18

God is love.

Ο Θεός είναι αγάπη.

O Theós eínai agápi.

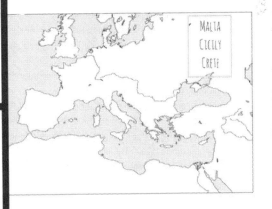

MALTA
CICILY
CRETE

BIBLE FACTS
REVIEW!

Paul's Journeys

Go! Let's go 'round the Mediterranean,
Go! Let's go with the Gospel and Paul,
Go! Let's go all around the world,
Telling everybody that Jesus is Lord.

On the road to Damascus,
Paul met Jesus alive!
Never would be the same again,
Once the scales had cleared from his eyes.

Paul and Silas in prison,
Chained up to a wall,
Singing out their hearts with joy,
Knowing Jesus was in control.

Started out from Antioch,
Spreading Jesus' word.
Four long journeys later he's in Rome
And thousands of people have heard!

Shipwrecked, beaten, stoned and more -
always carrying on.
Sharing Jesus everywhere-
Knowing he's for everyone!

Jesus' Sayings on the Cross

- Father, forgive them, for they know not what they do.
- I tell you the truth today, you'll be with Me in paradise.
- Woman, here's your son; here is your mother.
- My God, My god, why have You forsaken Me?
- I thirst.
- It is finished.
- Father, into Your hands I commit My spirit.

TIMELINE

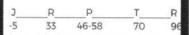

Paul writes more letters from prison

Titus sacks the Temple

Revelation vision

J	R	P	T	R
-5	33	46-58	70	96

hymn

COME, YE THANKFUL PEOPLE, COME
verse 4

Even so, Lord, quickly come,
bring Thy final harvest home;
gather Thou Thy people in,
free from sorrow, free from sin,
there, forever purified,
in Thy presence to abide:
come, with all Thine angels, come,
raise the glorious harvest home.

I PRACTICED:

☆ ☆ ☆ ☆ ☆ ☆

M	T	W	T	F	S
O	U	E	H	R	A
N	E	D	U	I	T

CYCLE 6
REVELATION VISION
WEEK 12

Philippians 2:1-11

REVIEW!

related stories

Revelation 1-22

Vos
New Testament
Lesson 92

Hurlbut Part 7
Lessons 20-21

In the beginning was the Word,
and the Word was with God
and God was the Word.

Ἐν ἀρχῇ ἦν
ὁ λόγος,
καὶ ὁ λόγος ἦν
πρὸς τὸν θεόν,
καὶ θεὸς ἦν
ὁ λόγος

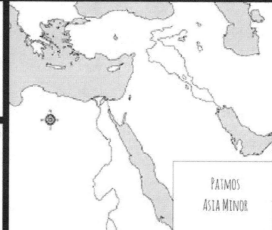

Patmos
Asia Minor

Old Testament Timeline

Creation, Fall, Cain and Abel,
Flood, Job, Tower of Babel,
Abraham, Ishmael,
Sodom and Gomorrah, Isaac as Well.

Jacob and Esau, Israel's Tribes,
Joseph in Egypt, Moses' Life,
Burning Bush and Plagues in Egypt,
Exodus and Ten Commandments,

Desert, Ark, Feasts, Tabernacle,
Joshua's Conquest, Judges Rule,
Ruth and Boaz, King Saul's Reign,
David's Kingdom, Psalms, Covenant.

Solomon's Temple, Kingdom Divides,
Ahab and Elijah on the North Side,
Hezekiah and Isaiah in the South,
Israel Falls to Assyria's Clout.

Jeremiah and Ezekiel Warn Judah,
Judah Falls To Babylon,
Temple Ruined
Daniel in the Exile, Cyrus' Decree,
Exiles Return, Temple Rebuilding.

Esther Saves the Jews,
Nehemiah Builds the Wall,
Malachi Foretells John the Baptist's Call,
Maccabean Period Ends Here,
No Word from God for 400 Years.

Feasts of the Lord

Passover: Saved by the blood of the lamb,
Unleavened Bread: Dead to sin, I am
Firstfruits: Celebrates life from the ground
Pentecost: Making laws and vows
Rosh Hashanah: New Year trumpets play
Yom Kippur: Atonement day
Tabernacles: Joy and peace
These are God's Appointed Feasts

Covenants

God made many promises called covenants,
The first, the Adamic, says a Savior will be sent,
Noahic says there won't again be sent
A flood to destroy the earth.

Abrahamic Covenant pledged at God's
command:
A great name, a nation, and a promised land,
Descendants just as numerous as sand,
A blessing to all the earth.

Mosaic says obey the law and you'll be fine,
Davidic: an eternal king from David's line,
New Covenant: I will make this people mine
God's promise to all the earth!

Hymns

Jesus Paid It All
A Mighty Fortress Is Our God
Crown Him with Many Crowns

Plagues in Egypt

Water (to blood)
Frogs
Gnats
Flies
Cattle
Boils
Hail
Locusts
Darkness
Death (of the firstborn)

Hebrew Alphabet

Handy Hebrew Writing Guide • Block Printing

Exodus 20:2-17

I am the Lord your God, who brought you out of Egypt, out of the land of slavery.

You shall have no other gods before Me.

You shall not make for yourself an image in the form of anything in heaven above or on the earth beneath or in the waters below. You shall not bow down to them or worship them; for I, the Lord your God, am a jealous God, punishing the children for the sin of the parents to the third and fourth generation of those who hate Me, but showing love to a thousand generations of those who love Me and keep My commandments.

You shall not misuse the name of the Lord your God, for the Lord will not hold anyone guiltless who misuses His name.

Remember the Sabbath day by keeping it holy. Six days you shall labor and do all your work, but the seventh day is a sabbath to the Lord your God. On it you shall not do any work, neither you, nor your son or daughter, nor your male or female servant, nor your animals, nor any foreigner residing in your towns. For in six days the Lord made the heavens and the earth, the sea, and all that is in them, but He rested on the seventh day. Therefore the Lord blessed the Sabbath day and made it holy.

Honor your father and your mother, so that you may live long in the land the Lord your God is giving you.

You shall not murder.

You shall not commit adultery.

You shall not steal.

You shall not give false testimony against your neighbor.

You shall not covet your neighbor's house. You shall not covet your neighbor's wife, or his male or female servant, his ox or donkey, or anything that belongs to your neighbor.

The Shema

Hear, O Israel, Yahweh our God,
Yahweh is one.
Blessed be the name of His
glorious kingdom forever and
ever.

שְׁמַע יִשְׂרָאֵל יהוה אֱלֹהֵינוּ יהוה אֶחָד
בָּרוּךְ שֵׁם כְּבוֹד מַלְכוּתוֹ לְעוֹלָם וָעֶד

Shema, Yisrael, Yahweh
eloheynu, Yahweh echad.

Barukh shem kevod malkuto
l'olam va-ed.

New Testament Timeline

John the Baptist, Messiah Is Born,
Shepherds and Magi Visit the Lord,
Flight into Egypt, Herod's Slaughter,
Boy Jesus at the Temple,
Baptism at the Jordan.

Temptation in the Desert,
Disciples' Call, Cana Wedding,
Jubilee Inaugural
Jesus Clears the Temple,
Ministry Begins.
Meets Nicodemus and the Samaritan.

Sermon on the Mount,
Jesus Feeds 5000,
Transfiguration, Miracles Abounding,
Parables, Triumphal Entry,
Olivet Discourse on Things to Be.

Last Passover, Crucifixion,
Resurrection, Ascension,
Pentecost, Holy Spirit Received,
Peter Preaches, 3000 Believe.

Stephen Martyred, Conversion of Saul,
Paul's First Journey, Jerusalem Council,
Paul's Second Journey, Thessalonians,
Romans, Galatians, Corinthians.

Paul Sent to Prison, Paul Stands Trial,
Paul Shipwrecked on an Isle,
Paul Writes More Letters from Prison,
Titus Sacks the Temple,
Revelation Vision.

Names of Jesus

Go! Let's go 'round the Mediterranean,
Go! Let's go with the Gospel and Paul,
Go! Let's go all around the world,
Telling everybody that Jesus is Lord.

On the road to Damascus,
Paul met Jesus alive!
Never would be the same again,
Once the scales had cleared from his eyes.

Paul and Silas in prison,
Chained up to a wall,
Singing out their hearts with joy,
Knowing Jesus was in control.

Started out from Antioch,
Spreading Jesus' word,
Four long journeys later he's in Rome
And thousands of people have heard!

Shipwrecked, beaten, stoned and more -
always carrying on.
Sharing Jesus everywhere-
Knowing He's for everyone!

Hymns

Come Thou Fount of Every Blessing
How Firm a Foundation
Come, Ye Thankful People, Come

Greek Alphabet

New Testament
MASTERY REVIEW
Cycle 6
6

1 John 4:16

God is love.

ο Θεός είναι αγάπη.

O Theós eínai agápi.

John 1:1

In the beginning was the Word,
and the Word was with God,
and God was the Word.

Ἐν ἀρχῇ ἦν ὁ λόγος,
καὶ ὁ λόγος ἦν πρὸς τὸν θεόν,
καὶ θεὸς ἦν ὁ λόγος

En ar-KAY ayn ha LOH-gohs,
kï ha LOH-gohs ayn pros ton theos,
kï theos nee LOH-gohs.

Philippians 2:1-11

If you have any encouragement
from being united with Christ, if
any comfort from His love, if any
fellowship with the Spirit, if any
tenderness and compassion,

then make my joy complete by
being like-minded, having the
same love, being one in spirit and
purpose.

Do nothing out of selfish ambition
or vain conceit, but in humility
consider others better than
yourselves.

Each of you should look not only to
your own interests, but also to the
interests of others.

Your attitude should be the same
as that of Christ Jesus:

Who, being in very nature God, did
not consider equality with God
something to be grasped,

but made Himself nothing, taking
the very nature of a servant, being
made in human likeness.

And being found in appearance as
a man, He humbled Himself and
became obedient to death-- even
death on a cross!

Therefore God exalted Him to the
highest place and gave Him the
name that is above every name,

that at the name of Jesus every
knee should bow, in heaven and on
earth and under the earth,

and every tongue confess that
Jesus Christ is Lord, to the glory of
God the Father.

Jesus' Sayings on the Cross

- Father, forgive them, for they
  know not what they do.
- I tell you the truth today, you'll
  be with Me in paradise.
- Woman, here's your son; here is
  your mother.
- My God, My god, why have You
  forsaken Me?
- I thirst.
- It is finished.
- Father, into Your hands I commit
  My spirit.

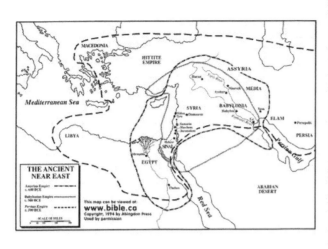

THE ANCIENT
NEAR EAST

Assyrian Empire
c. 650 BCE
Babylonian Empire
c. 500 BCE
Persian Empire
c. 500 BCE

SCALE OF MILES

This map can be viewed at:
www.bible.ca
Copyright, 1994 by Abingdon Press
Used by permission

This map can be viewed at:
www.bible.ca

Israel
at the
Time of Christ
30 AD

SCALE OF MILES

The Great Sea
(Mediterranean Sea)

This map can be viewed at:
www.bible.ca
Copyright, 1994 by Abingdon Press
Used by permission

PAUL'S
FIRST JOURNEY
Acts 13:1-14:28

SCALE OF MILES

Classical
Sunday School

FAMILY DRILL BOOK
CYCLES 7 & 8

To learn more about Classical education, and for
great tips on using this Drill Book, go to
StrongHappyFamily.org

BIBLE FACTS

The Tabernacle

To the tune of "If You're Happy and You Know It"

Inside the Tabernacle:
Were Bronze Altar and
Lampstand of gold
Mercy Seat, Bronze Laver,
And the Showbread table
Ark of Covenant
Incense Altar of gold.

TIMELINE

Creation

Fall

Cain and Abel

hymn

WHAT A FRIEND
WE HAVE IN JESUS
verse 1

What a friend we have in Jesus,
all our sins and griefs to bear!
What a privilege to carry
everything to God in prayer!
O what peace we often forfeit,
O what needless pain we bear,
all because we do not carry
everything to God in prayer!

I PRACTICED:

☆ ☆ ☆ ☆ ☆
M T W T F S
O U E H R A
N E D U I T

CYCLE 7
CREATION
WEEK 1

Deuteronomy 6:4

Hear, O Israel: The
Lord our God, the
Lord is one.

related stories

Genesis 1-2

Vos Old
Testament
Lessons 1-4

Hurlbut Part 1
Lesson 1

Aleph
א

Bet
ב

GREAT SEA
CANAAN
EGYPT
MESOPOTAMIA

BIBLE FACTS

The Tabernacle

To the tune of "If You're Happy and You Know It"

Inside the Tabernacle:
Were Bronze Altar and
Lampstand of gold
Mercy Seat, Bronze Laver,
And the Showbread table
Ark of Covenant
Incense Altar of gold.

TIMELINE

Flood

Job

Tower of
Babel

hymn

WHAT A FRIEND
WE HAVE IN JESUS
verse 2

Have we trials and temptations?
Is there trouble anywhere?
We should never be discouraged;
take it to the Lord in prayer!
Can we find a friend so faithful
Who will all our sorrows share?
Jesus knows our every weakness;
take it to the Lord in prayer!

I PRACTICED:

☆ ☆ ☆ ☆ ☆ ☆

M	T	W	T	F	S
O	U	E	H	R	A
N	E	D	U	I	T

CYCLE 7

FLOOD

WEEK 2

DEUTERONOMY 6:5

Love the Lord
your God

with all your heart

and with all your soul

and with all your
strength.

related stories

Genesis 6-9

Vos Old
Testament
Lesson 10

Hurlbut Part 1
Lessons 3-4

Gimel
ג

Dalet
ד

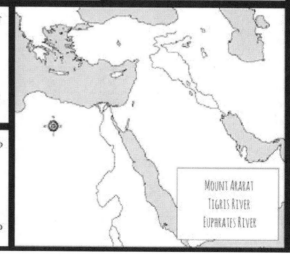

MOUNT ARARAT
TIGRIS RIVER
EUPHRATES RIVER

BIBLE FACTS

THE TABERNACLE

To the tune of "If You're Happy and You Know It"

Inside the Tabernacle:
Were Bronze Altar and
Lampstand of gold
Mercy Seat, Bronze Laver,
And the Showbread table
Ark of Covenant
Incense Altar of gold.

I PRACTICED:

☆ ☆ ☆ ☆ ☆

M	T	W	T	F	S
O	U	E	H	R	A
N	E	D	U	I	T

CYCLE 7
ABRAHAM
WEEK 3

TIMELINE

Abraham

Ishmael

Sodom and Gomorrah

A	M	D	E
2000	1500	1000	500

hymn

WHAT A FRIEND
WE HAVE IN JESUS
verse 3

Are we weak and heavy laden,
cumbered with a load of care?
Precious Savior, still our refuge--
take it to the Lord in prayer!
Do your friends despise, forsake you?
Take it to the Lord in prayer!
In His arms He'll take and shield you;
you wilt find a solace there.

Deuteronomy 6:6

These commandments that I give you today are to be on your hearts.

related stories

Genesis 12-25

Vos Old
Testament
Lesson 12

Hurlbut Part 1
Lesson 5

He
ה

Vav
ו

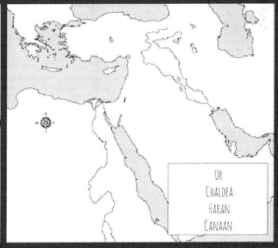

UR
CHALDEA
HARAN
CANAAN

BIBLE FACTS

The Tabernacle

To the tune of "If You're Happy and You Know It"

Inside the Tabernacle:
Were Bronze Altar and
Lampstand of gold
Mercy Seat, Bronze Laver,
And the Showbread table
Ark of Covenant
Incense Altar of gold.

TIMELINE

Isaac as well

Jacob and Esau

Israel's tribes

A	M	D	E
2000	1500	1000	500

hymn

O WORSHIP THE KING
verse 1

O worship the King
all-glorious above,
O gratefully sing
His power and His love:
Our shield and defender,
the Ancient of Days,
pavilioned in splendor
and girded with praise.

I PRACTICED:

☆ ☆ ☆ ☆ ☆ ☆

M	T	W	T	F	S
O	U	E	H	R	A
N	E	D	U	I	T

CYCLE 7
ISAAC
WEEK 4

Deuteronomy 6:7

Impress them
on your children.
Talk about them
when you sit at home
and when you walk
along the road,
when you lie down
and when you get up.

related stories

Genesis 21-29

Vos Old
Testament
Lessons 16-17

Hurlbut Part 1
Lessons 10-11

Zayin
т

Het
n

SEA OF GALILEE
JORDAN RIVER
DEAD SEA

BIBLE FACTS

Names for Yahweh, v. 1

To the Tune of "Away in a Manger"

Elohim: Creator, El Roi: God who Sees,

El Shaddai means God Almighty,

Jehovah Nissi: The Lord our Banner,

Jehovah Rohi: The Lord our Shepherd.

TIMELINE

Joseph in Egypt

Moses' Life

Burning bush
and plagues in
Egypt

<u>_A_</u>____<u>M</u>____<u>D</u>____<u>E</u>__
2000   1500   1000   500

hymn

O WORSHIP THE KING
verse 2

O tell of His might
and sing of His grace,
Whose robe is the light,
Whose canopy space.
His chariots of wrath
the deep thunderclouds form,
and dark is His path
on the wings of the storm.

I PRACTICED:

☆ ☆ ☆ ☆ ☆

M	T	W	T	F	S
O	U	E	H	R	A
N	E	D	U	I	T

CYCLE 7
JOSEPH
WEEK 5

Deuteronomy 6:8

Tie them as symbols
on your hands

and bind them on
your foreheads.

related stories

Genesis 37-50

Vos Old
Testament
Lessons 24-31

Hurlbut Part 1
Lessons 15-19

Tet
ט

Yod
י

MIDIAN
GOSHEN
NILE RIVER
EGYPT

BIBLE FACTS

Names for Yahweh, v. 2

To the tune of "Away in a Manger"

Jehovah Jirah: The Lord Will Provide,

El El-yon means God Most High,

El Olam means God Everlasting,

Jehovah Rapha: The Lord who Heals.

TIMELINE

Exodus and 10 Commandments

Desert, Ark, Feasts, Tabernacle

Joshua's Conquest

A	M	D	E
2000	1500	1000	500

hymn

O WORSHIP THE KING
verse 3

Your bountiful care,
what tongue can recite?
It breathes in the air,
t shines in the light;
it streams from the hills,
it descends to the plain,
and sweetly distills
in the dew and the rain.

I PRACTICED:

☆ ☆ ☆ ☆ ☆ ☆

M	T	W	T	F	S
O	U	E	H	R	A
N	E	D	U	I	T

CYCLE 7
Exodus and Law
WEEK 6

Deuteronomy 6:9

Write them
on the doorframes
of your houses
and on your gates.

related stories

Exodus 12-20

Vos Old Testament Lessons 35-39

Hurlbut Part 1 Lessons 24-26

Kaf
כ

Lamed
ל

Red Sea
Mount Sinai
Sinai Desert

BIBLE FACTS

Names for Yahweh, v. 3

To the tune of "Away In a Manger"

Jehovah Shalom: The Lord is our Peace,

Adonai means Lord Almighty,

Your Sanctifier: Jehovah Maccaddeshem,

Jehovah Tsidkenu: Our righteousness.

TIMELINE

Judges rule

Ruth and Boaz

King Saul's reign

A_____M_____D_____E__
2000   1500   1000   500

hymn

O WORSHIP THE KING
verse 4

Frail children of dust,
and feeble as frail,
in You do we trust,
nor find You to fail.
Your mercies, how tender,
how firm to the end,
our Maker, Defender,
Redeemer, and Friend!

I PRACTICED:

☆ ☆ ☆ ☆ ☆
M T W T F S
O U E H R A
N E D U I T

CYCLE 7
Judges rule
WEEK 7

Psalm 23:1

The Lord is
my shepherd;

I shall not want.

related stories

Judges 1-21

Vos Old Testament
Lessons 57-63

Hurlbut Part 2
Lessons 6-17

Mem

ﬦ
ם

EDOM
MOAB
AMMON
PHILISTIA
GAZA

BIBLE FACTS

Names for Yahweh, v. 4

To the tune of "Away in a Manger"

Jehovah Sabbaoth: Lord of Hosts

everywhere,

Jehovah Shammah: The Lord who is there,

Abba means Pappa, Mighty God: El Gibhor,

Speak reverently,

these are the Names of the Lord.

TIMELINE

David's Kingdom

Psalms, Covenant

Solomon's Temple,
Kingdom divides

A	M	D	E
2000	1500	1000	500

hymn

O WORSHIP THE KING
verse 5

O measureless Might,
unchangeable Love,
Whom angels delight
to worship above!
Your ransomed creation,
with glory ablaze,
in true adoration
shall sing to Your praise!

I PRACTICED:

☆ ☆ ☆ ☆ ☆ ☆

M	T	W	T	F	S
O	U	E	H	R	A
N	E	D	U	I	T

CYCLE 7
David's Kingdom
WEEK 8

Psalm 23:2

He maketh me to
lie down in green
pastures:

He leadeth me
beside the still
waters.

related stories

2 Samuel 1-24
1 Kings 1-2

Vos Old
Testament
Lessons 72-75

Hurlbut Part 3
Lessons 10-16

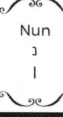

Nun

ב

נ

Jerusalem
Bethlehem
Philistia
Gath
Tyre and Sidon

BIBLE FACTS

Old Testament Offerings

To the tune of "Michael Finnegan"

Peace or fellowship offerings,

Meal/grain offerings,

Burnt offerings,

Trespass or guilt offerings,

Sin offerings.

TIMELINE

Ahab and Elijah on the north side

Hezekiah and Isaiah in the South

Israel falls to Assyria's clout

A	M	D	E
2000	1500	1000	500

hymn

AMERICA THE BEAUTIFUL
verse 1

O beautiful for spacious skies,
For amber waves of grain;
For purple mountain majesties
Above the fruited plain!
America! America!
God shed His grace on thee,
And crown thy good
with brotherhood
From sea to shining sea!

I PRACTICED:

☆ ☆ ☆ ☆ ☆ ☆

M	T	W	T	F	S
O	U	E	H	R	A
N	E	D	U	I	T

CYCLE 7
Ahab and Elijah
WEEK 9

Psalm 23:3

He restoreth my soul:
He leadeth me
in the paths of
righteousness
for His name's sake.

related stories

1 Kings 17-22
2 Kings 1-2

Vos Old Testament Lessons 80-89

Hurlbut Part 4 Lessons 2-16

Samekh
ס
Ayin
ע

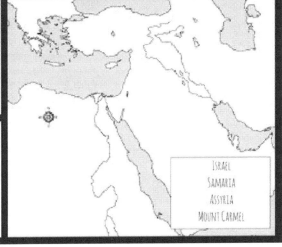

Israel
Samaria
Assyria
Mount Carmel

BIBLE FACTS
Old Testament Offerings
To the tune of "Michael Finnegan"

Peace or fellowship offerings,

Meal/grain offerings,

Burnt offerings,

Trespass or guilt offerings,

Sin offerings.

TIMELINE

Jeremiah and Ezekiel
warn Judah

Judah falls to Babylon,
Temple ruined

Daniel in the Exile

_A____ ____M____ ____D___ __E__
2000   1500   1000   500

---

hymn

AMERICA THE BEAUTIFUL
verse 2

O beautiful for pilgrim feet,
Whose stern, impassioned stress
A thoroughfare for freedom beat
Across the wilderness!
America! America!
God mend thine ev'ry flaw,
Confirm thy soul in self-control,
Thy liberty in law!

I PRACTICED:

☆ ☆ ☆ ☆ ☆ ☆
M T W T F S
O U E H R A
N E D U I T
  N D U I T

CYCLE 7
Jeremiah and Ezekiel
WEEK 10

Psalm 23:4

Yea, though I walk
through the valley
of the shadow of death,
I will fear no evil:
for Thou art with me;
Thy rod and Thy staff
they comfort me.

---

related stories

Jeremiah 1-52
Ezekiel 1-48

Vos Old
Testament
Lessons 98-99

Hurlbut Part 5
Lessons 1-18

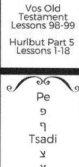

Pe
פ
ף
Tsadi
צ
ץ

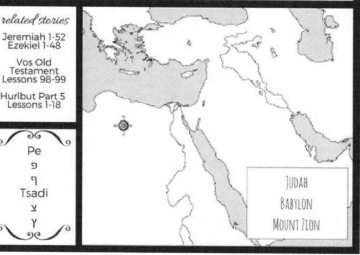

Judah
Babylon
Mount Zion

BIBLE FACTS

Old Testament Offerings
To the tune of "Michael Finnegan"

Peace or fellowship offerings,

Meal/grain offerings,

Burnt offerings,

Trespass or guilt offerings,

Sin offerings.

TIMELINE

Cyrus' decree
Exiles return

Temple rebuilding

Esther saves the
Jews

A	M	D	E
2000	1500	1000	500

hymn

AMERICA THE BEAUTIFUL
verse 3

O beautiful for heroes proved
In liberating strife,
Who more than self
their country loved,
And mercy more than life!
America! America!
May God thy gold refine,
Till all success be nobleness
And every gain divine!

I PRACTICED:

☆ ☆ ☆ ☆ ☆

M	T	W	T	F	S
O	U	E	H	R	A
N	E	D	U	I	T

CYCLE 7

Cyrus' Decree

WEEK 11

Psalm 23:5

Thou preparest a table
before me
in the presence of
mine enemies:
Thou anointest
my head with oil;
my cup runneth over.

related stories

Ezra 5

Vos Old
Testament
Lessons 105-106

Hurlbut Part 5
Lesson 13

Qof
ק

Resh
ר

Caspian Sea
Black Sea
Persia
Jerusalem

BIBLE FACTS

Old Testament Offerings

To the tune of "Michael Finnegan"

Peace or fellowship offerings,

Meal/grain offerings,

Burnt offerings,

Trespass or guilt offerings,

Sin offerings.

TIMELINE

Nehemiah builds the wall

Malachi foretells John the Baptist's call

Maccabean period ends here, no word from God for 400 years

_A_	_M_	_D_	_E_
2000	1500	1000	500

hymn

AMERICA THE BEAUTIFUL
verse 4

O beautiful for patriot dream
That sees beyond the years
Thine alabaster cities gleam
Undimmed by human tears!
America! America!
God shed His grace on thee.
And crown thy good
with brotherhood
From sea to shining sea!

I PRACTICED:

☆ ☆ ☆ ☆ ☆ ☆

M	T	W	T	F	S
O	U	E	H	R	A
N	E	D	U	I	T

CYCLE 7

Nehemiah builds the wall

WEEK 12

Psalm 23:6

Surely goodness
and mercy
shall follow me
all the days of my life:
and I will dwell
in the house of the Lord
for ever.

related stories

Nehemiah 1-13

Vos Old Testament Lesson 110

Hurlbut Part 5 Lesson 17

Shin
ש

Tav
ת

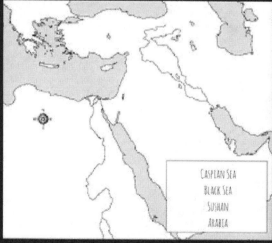

Caspian Sea
Black Sea
Sushan
Arabia

BIBLE FACTS
MIRACLES OF JESUS
TO THE TUNE OF "OLD MACDONALD"

The Lord turned water into wine,

Healed the sick, deaf, dumb and blind.

Cast out demons, calmed the sea,

Raised the dead, killed a tree.

Healed the lame, cured leprosy,

Restored a withered limb and a severed ear,

Two enormous crowds He fed,

Walked on water, rose from the dead.

TIMELINE

John the Baptist

Messiah is born

Shepherds and
Magi visit the Lord

J	R	P	T	R
-5	33	46-58	70	96

hymn

THE OLD RUGGED CROSS
verse 1

On a hill far away
stood an old rugged cross,
the emblem of suffering and shame;
and I love that old cross
where the dearest and best
for a world of lost sinners was slain.

Refrain:
So I'll cherish the old rugged cross,
till my trophies at last I lay down;
I will cling to the old rugged cross,
and exchange it some day
for a crown.

I PRACTICED:

☆ ☆ ☆ ☆ ☆ ☆

M	T	W	T	F	S
O	U	E	H	R	A
N	E	D	U	I	T

CYCLE 8

John the Baptist

WEEK 1

JOHN 1:1-2

In the beginning
was the Word,

and the Word
was with God,

and the Word was God.

He was with God
in the beginning.

related stories

Luke 1

Vos New
Testament
Lessons 1 & 25

Hurlbut Part 6
Lessons 1, 5, 18

Alpha
A α

Beta
B β

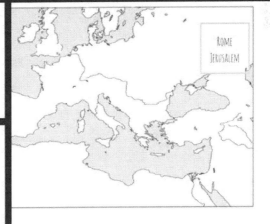

BIBLE FACTS

Miracles of Jesus

To the tune of "Old MacDonald"

The Lord turned water into wine,

Healed the sick, deaf, dumb and blind.

Cast out demons, calmed the sea,

Raised the dead, killed a tree.

Healed the lame, cured leprosy,

Restored a withered limb and a severed ear.

Two enormous crowds He fed,

Walked on water, rose from the dead.

TIMELINE

Flight into Egypt
Herod's Slaughter

Boy Jesus at the Temple

Baptism at the Jordan

J	R	P	T	R
-5	33	46-58	70	96

hymn

THE OLD RUGGED CROSS
verse 2

O that old rugged cross,
so despised by the world,
has a wondrous attraction for me;
for the dear Lamb of God
left His glory above
to bear it to dark Calvary.

Refrain
So I'll cherish the old rugged cross,
till my trophies at last I lay down;
I will cling to the old rugged cross,
and exchange it some day
for a crown.

I PRACTICED:

☆ ☆ ☆ ☆ ☆ ☆

M	T	W	T	F	S
O	U	E	H	R	A
N	E	D	U	I	T

CYCLE 8
Flight into Egypt
WEEK 2

JOHN 1:3-4

Through Him
all things were made;

without Him
nothing was made
that has been made.

In Him was life,

and that life
was the light
of all mankind.

related stories

Matthew 2

Vos New
Testament
Lessons 4-5

Hurlbut Part 6
Lesson 3

Gamma
Γ γ

Delta
Δ δ

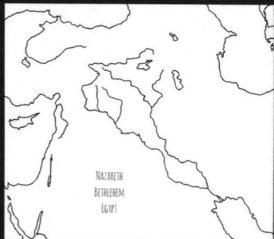

Nazareth
Bethlehem
Egypt

BIBLE FACTS

MIRACLES OF JESUS

TO THE TUNE OF "OLD MACDONALD"

The Lord turned water into wine,

Healed the sick, deaf, dumb and blind.

Cast out demons, calmed the sea,

Raised the dead, killed a tree.

Healed the lame, cured leprosy,

Restored a withered limb and a severed ear,

Two enormous crowds He fed,

Walked on water, rose from the dead.

TIMELINE

Temptation in the desert

Disciples' Call

Cana Wedding
Jubilee Inaugural

J	R	P	T	R
-5	33	46-58	70	96

hymn

THE OLD RUGGED CROSS
verse 3

In that old rugged cross,
stained with blood so divine,
a wondrous beauty I see,
for 'twas on that old cross
Jesus suffered and died,
to pardon and sanctify me.

Refrain:
So I'll cherish the old rugged cross,
till my trophies at last I lay down;
I will cling to the old rugged cross,
and exchange it some day
for a crown

I PRACTICED:

☆ ☆ ☆ ☆ ☆ ☆

M	T	W	T	F	S
O	U	E	H	R	A
N	E	D	U	I	T

CYCLE 8

Temptation in the Desert

WEEK 3

JOHN 1:5

The light shines
in the darkness,

and the darkness
has not
overcome it.

related stories

Matthew 4
Luke 4

Vos New
Testament
Lesson 8

Hurlbut Part 6
Lesson 6

Epsilon
E ε

Zeta
Z ζ

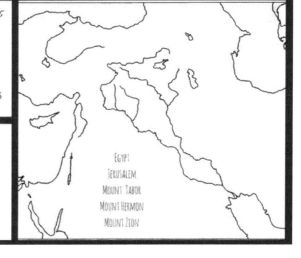

Egypt
Jerusalem
Mount Tabor
Mount Hermon
Mount Zion

BIBLE FACTS

MIRACLES OF JESUS
TO THE TUNE OF "OLD MACDONALD"

The Lord turned water into wine,

Healed the sick, deaf, dumb and blind.

Cast out demons, calmed the sea,

Raised the dead, killed a tree.

Healed the lame, cured leprosy,

Restored a withered limb and a severed ear.

Two enormous crowds He fed,

Walked on water, rose from the dead.

TIMELINE

Jesus clears the Temple, Ministry begins

Meets Nicodemus and the Samaritan

Sermon on the Mount

J	R	P	T	R
-5	33	46-58	70	96

hymn

THE OLD RUGGED CROSS
verse 4

To that old rugged cross
I will ever be true,
its shame and reproach gladly bear;
then He'll call me some day
to my home far away,
where His glory forever I'll share.

Refrain:
So I'll cherish the old rugged cross,
till my trophies at last I lay down;
I will cling to the old rugged cross,
and exchange it some day for a crown.

I PRACTICED:

☆ ☆ ☆ ☆ ☆ ☆

M	T	W	T	F	S
O	U	E	H	R	A
N	E	D	U	I	T

CYCLE 8
Jesus' ministry begins
WEEK 4

JOHN 1:6

There was a man sent from God

whose name was John.

related stories
John 2

Vos New Testament
Lessons 11, 18, 34-36, 40, 42

Hurlbut Part 6
Lessons 7, 10-12, 21-23, 29, 31

Eta
H η

Theta
Θ θ

Nazareth
Galilee
Jerusalem

BIBLE FACTS

ATTRIBUTES OF GOD, V. 1

TO THE TUNE OF "THE WHEELS ON THE BUS"

God's eternal, infinite,

Self-existent, self-sufficient,

God is omnipresent

And omniscient.

TIMELINE

Jesus feeds 5000,

Transfiguration,

Miracles abounding

J	R	P	T	R
-5	33	46-58	70	96

hymn

AND CAN IT BE?
verse 1

And can it be that I should gain
An int'rest in the Savior's blood?
Died He for me, who caused His pain?
For me, who Him to death pursued?
Amazing love! how can it be
That Thou, my God, should die for me?

Refrain:
Amazing love! how can it be
That Thou, my God, should die for me!

I PRACTICED:

☆ ☆ ☆ ☆ ☆ ☆

M	T	W	T	F	S
O	U	E	H	R	A
N	E	D	U	I	T

CYCLE 8

Jesus feeds 5000

WEEK 5

JOHN 1:7

He came as a witness
to testify concerning
that light,

so that through Him
all might believe.

related stories

Matthew 14,
John 6, Mark 8

Vos New
Testament
Lessons 26, 30

Hurlbut Part 6
Lesson 19

Iota
I ι

Kappa
K κ

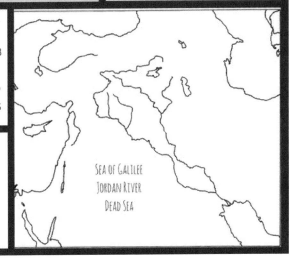

Sea of Galilee
Jordan River
Dead Sea

BIBLE FACTS

Attributes of God, v.2
To the tune of "The Wheels on the Bus"

God is immutable,

Sovereign, wise, holy, good,

Righteous, just, faithful and true

God is triune.

TIMELINE

Parables
Triumphal Entry
Olivet Discourse on
things to be

J	R	P		T	R
-5	33	46-58		70	96

hymn

AND CAN IT BE?
verse 2

'Tis mystery all! Th'Immortal dies!
Who can explore His strange design?
In vain the firstborn seraph tries
To sound the depths of love divine!
'Tis mercy all! let earth adore,
Let angel minds inquire no more.

Refrain:
Amazing love! how can it be
That Thou, my God, should die for me!

I PRACTICED:

☆ ☆ ☆ ☆ ☆ ☆

M	T	W	T	F	S
O	U	E	H	R	A
N	E	D	U	I	T

CYCLE 8
Parables
WEEK 6

JOHN 1:8

He himself was not
the light;

he came only as a
witness to the light.

related stories
Luke 10-20

Vos New
Testament
Lessons 22, 33, 37

Hurlbut Part 6
Lessons 15, 25, 27,
28

Lambda
Λ λ

Mu
M μ

Sea of Galilee
Bethsaida
Capernaum

BIBLE FACTS

ATTRIBUTES OF GOD, V. 3
TO THE TUNE OF "THE WHEELS ON THE BUS"

God is gracious, merciful,

He is spirit, and life too,

God is omnipresent,

God is love, it's true!

TIMELINE

Last Passover

Crucifixion

Resurrection

J	R	P	T	R
-5	33	46-58	70	96

hymn

AND CAN IT BE?
verse 3

He left His Father's throne above,
So free, so infinite His grace;
Emptied Himself of all but love,
And bled for Adam's helpless race;
Tis mercy all, immense and free;
For, O my God, it found out me.

Refrain:
Amazing love! how can it be
That Thou, my God,
should die for me!

I PRACTICED:

☆ ☆ ☆ ☆ ☆

M	T	W	T	F	S
O	U	E	H	R	A
N	E	D	U	I	T

CYCLE 8
Last Passover
WEEK 7

JOHN 1:9

The true light

that gives light
to everyone

was coming
into the world.

related stories
Mark 26, Luke 22

Vos New
Testament
Lessons 44, 45

Hurlbut Part 6
Lessons 33, 34

Nu
N ν

Xi
Ξ ξ

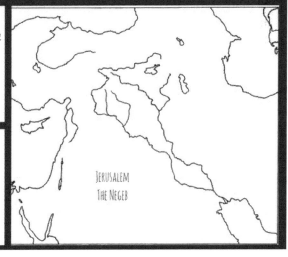

Jerusalem
The Negeb

BIBLE FACTS

Attributes of God
To the tune of "The Wheels on the Bus"

God's eternal, infinite,
Self-existent, self-sufficient,
God is omnipresent,
And omniscient.

Good is immutable,
Sovereign, wise, holy, good,
Righteous, just, faithful and true,
God is triune.

God is gracious, merciful,
He is spirit and life too,
God is omnipotent,
God is love, it's true!

TIMELINE

Ascension

Pentecost, Holy Spirit received

Peter preaches, 3,000 believe

J	R	P	T	R
-5	33	46-58	70	96

hymn

AND CAN IT BE?
verse 4

Long my imprisoned spirit lay
Fast bound in sin and nature's night;
Thine eye diffused a quick'ning ray,
I woke, the dungeon flamed with light;
My chains fell off, my heart was free;
I rose, went forth and followed Thee.

Refrain:
Amazing love! how can it be
That Thou, my God, should die for me!

I PRACTICED:

☆ ☆ ☆ ☆ ☆ ☆

M	T	W	T	F	S
O	U	E	H	R	A
N	E	D	U	I	T

CYCLE 8
Ascension
WEEK 8

JOHN 1:10

He was in the world, and though the world was made through Him,

the world did not recognize Him.

related stories

Luke 24, Acts 1

Vos New Testament Lessons 55, 56

Hurlbut Part 6 Lesson 38

Omicron
O o

Pi
Π π

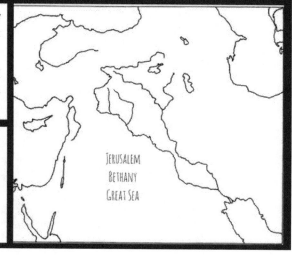

Jerusalem
Bethany
Great Sea

BIBLE FACTS
Churches of Revelation
To the Tune of "This Old Man"

Revelation churches are:

Ephesus, Smyrna, Pergamon,

Thyatira, Sardis, Philadelphia,

Laodicea, seven in all!

TIMELINE

Stephen martyred

Conversion of Saul

Paul's first journey

J	R	P	T	R
-5	33	46-58	70	96

hymn

AND CAN IT BE?
verse 5

No condemnation now I dread:
Jesus, and all in Him is mine!
Alive in Him, my living Head,
And clothed in righteousness divine,
Bold I approach th'eternal throne,
And claim the crown,
through Christ my own.

Refrain:
Amazing love! how can it be
That Thou, my God, should die for me!

I PRACTICED:
☆ ☆ ☆ ☆ ☆ ☆

M	T	W	T	F	S
O	U	E	H	R	A
N	E	D	U	I	T

CYCLE 8
Stephen martyred
WEEK 9

JOHN 1:11

He came to that
which was His own,

but His own
did not receive Him.

related stories

Acts 7

Vos New
Testament
Lessons 61, 63

Hurlbut Part 7
Lesson 4

Rho
P ρ

Sigma
Σ σ

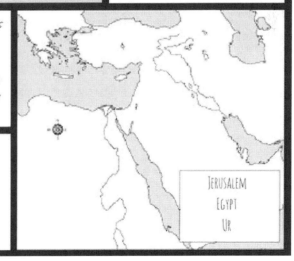

Jerusalem
Egypt
Ur

BIBLE FACTS

CHURCHES OF REVELATION
TO THE TUNE OF "THIS OLD MAN"

Revelation churches are:

Ephesus, Smyrna, Pergamon,

Thyatira, Sardis, Philadelphia,

Laodicea, seven in all!

TIMELINE

Jerusalem Council

Paul's Second Journey

Thessalonians, Galatians, Romans, Corinthians

J	R	P	T	R
-5	33	46-58	70	96

hymn

BE STILL MY SOUL
verse 1

Be still, my soul: the Lord is on thy side.
Bear patiently the cross of grief or pain.
Leave to thy God to order and provide.
Who through all changes
faithful will remain.

Be still, my soul:
thy best, thy heavenly Friend
through thorny ways
leads to a joyful end.

I PRACTICED:

☆ ☆ ☆ ☆ ☆ ☆

M	T	W	T	F	S
O	U	E	H	R	A
N	E	D	U	I	T

CYCLE 8
Jerusalem Council
WEEK 10

JOHN 1:12

Yet to all who did receive Him,

to those who believed in His name,

He gave the right to become children of God—

related stories

Acts 15

Vos New Testament Lessons 68, 69

Hurlbut Part 7 Lesson 10

Tau
T τ

Upsilon
Y υ

JERUSALEM
ANTIOCH
ATHENS

BIBLE FACTS

CHURCHES IN REVELATION
TO THE TUNE OF "THIS OLD MAN"

Revelation churches are:

Ephesus, Smyrna, Pergamon,

Thyatira, Sardis, Philadelphia,

Laodicea, seven in all!

TIMELINE

Paul sent to prison

Paul stands trial

Paul shipwrecked on an isle

J	R	P	T	R
-5	33	46-58	70	96

hymn

BE STILL MY SOUL
verse 2

Be still, my soul:
thy God doth undertake
to guide the future surely as the past.
Thy hope, thy confidence
let nothing shake;
all now mysterious shall be bright at last.

Be still, my soul:
the waves and winds still know
His voice who ruled them
while He dwelt below.

I PRACTICED:

☆ ☆ ☆ ☆ ☆ ☆
M T W T F S
O U E H R A
N E D U I T

CYCLE 8
Paul sent to prison
WEEK 11

JOHN 1:13

children born
not of natural descent,

nor of human decision
or a husband's will,

but born of God.

related stories
Acts 16, 27

Vos New
Testament
Lesson 91

Hurlbut Part 7
Lesson 16, 17

Phi
Φ φ

Chi
X χ

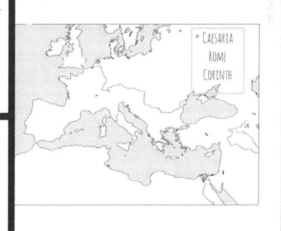

BIBLE FACTS
Churches in Revelation
to the tune of "This Old Man"

Revelation churches are:

Ephesus, Smyrna, Pergamon,

Thyatira, Sardis, Philadelphia,

Laodicea, seven in all!

TIMELINE

Paul writes more letters from prison

Titus sacks the Temple

Revelation vision

J	R	P	T	R
-5	33	46-58	70	96

hymn

BE STILL MY SOUL
verse 3

Be still, my soul: the hour is hastening on
when we shall be forever with the Lord;
when disappointment,
grief, and fear are gone,
sorrow forgot, love's purest joys restored.

Be still, my soul:
when change and tears are past
all safe and blessed
we shall meet at last.

I PRACTICED:

☆ ☆ ☆ ☆ ☆ ☆

M	T	W	T	F	S
O	U	E	H	R	A
N	E	D	U	I	T

CYCLE 8
Paul's Prison Letters
WEEK 12

JOHN 1:14

The Word became flesh
and made His dwelling
among us.

We have seen His glory,
the glory of
the one and only Son.

Who came from the Father,
full of grace and truth.

related stories

Ephesians,
Philippians,
Colossians,
Philemon

Hurlbut Part 7
Lesson 19

Psi
Ψ ψ

Omega
Ω ω

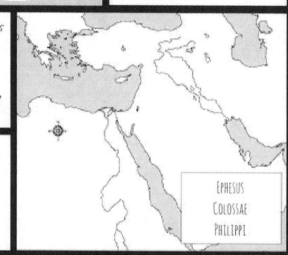

Ephesus
Colossae
Philippi

Old Testament Timeline

Creation, Fall, Cain and Abel,
Flood, Job, Tower of Babel,
Abraham, Ishmael,
Sodom and Gomorrah, Isaac as Well.

Jacob and Esau, Israel's Tribes,
Joseph in Egypt, Moses' Life,
Burning Bush and Plagues in Egypt,
Exodus and Ten Commandments,

Desert, Ark, Feasts, Tabernacle,
Joshua's Conquest, Judges Rule,
Ruth and Boaz, King Saul's Reign,
David's Kingdom, Psalms, Covenant.

Solomon's Temple, Kingdom Divides,
Ahab and Elijah on the North Side,
Hezekiah and Isaiah in the South,
Israel Falls to Assyria's Clout.

Jeremiah and Ezekiel Warn Judah,
Judah Falls To Babylon,
Temple Ruined
Daniel in the Exile, Cyrus' Decree,
Exiles Return, Temple Rebuilding.

Esther Saves the Jews,
Nehemiah Builds the Wall,
Malachi Foretells
John the Baptist's Call,
Maccabean Period Ends Here,
No Word from God for 400 Years.

Names for Yahweh

Elohim: Creator, El Roi: God who Sees,
El Shaddai means God Almighty,
Jehovah Nissi: The Lord our Banner,
Jehovah Rohi: The Lord our Shepherd.

Jehovah Jirah: The Lord Will Provide,
El El-yon means God Most High,
El Olam means God Everlasting,
Jehovah Rapha: The Lord who Heals.

Jehovah Shalom: The Lord is our Peace,
Adonai means Lord Almighty,
Your Sanctifier: Jehovah Maccaddeshem,
Jehovah Tsidkenu: Our righteousness.

Jehovah Sabbaoth: Lord of Hosts everywhere,
Jehovah Shammah: The Lord who is there,
Abba means Pappa, Mighty God: El Gibhor,
Speak reverently,
these are the names of the Lord.

Hymns

What a Friend We Have in Jesus
O Worship the King
America the Beautiful

Old Testament Offerings

Peace or fellowship offerings,
Meal/grain offerings,
Burnt offerings,
Trespass or guilt offerings,
Sin offerings.

The Tabernacle

Inside the Tabernacle:
Were Bronze Altar and
Lampstand of gold
Mercy Seat, Bronze Laver,
And the Showbread table
Ark of Covenant
Incense Altar of gold.

7
Old Testament
MASTERY REVIEW
Cycle 7

Hebrew Alphabet

Deuteronomy 6:4-9

Hear, O Israel: The Lord our God, the Lord is one.

Love the Lord your God with all your heart and with all your soul and with all your strength.

These commandments that I give you today are to be on your hearts.

Impress them on your children. Talk about them when you sit at home and when you walk along the road, when you lie down and when you get up.

Tie them as symbols on your hands and bind them on your foreheads.

Write them on the doorframes of your houses and on your gates.

Psalm 23

The Lord is my shepherd; I shall not want.

He maketh me to lie down in green pastures: He leadeth me beside the still waters.

He restoreth my soul: He leadeth me in the paths of righteousness for His name's sake.

Yea, though I walk through the valley of the shadow of death, I will fear no evil: for Thou art with me; Thy rod and Thy staff they comfort me.

Thou preparest a table before me in the presence of mine enemies: Thou anointest my head with oil; my cup runneth over.

Surely goodness and mercy shall follow me all the days of my life: and I will dwell in the house of the Lord for ever.

New Testament Timeline

John the Baptist, Messiah Is Born,
Shepherds and Magi Visit the Lord,
Flight into Egypt, Herod's Slaughter,
Boy Jesus at the Temple,
Baptism at the Jordan.

Temptation in the Desert,
Disciples' Call, Cana Wedding,
Jubilee Inaugural
Jesus Clears the Temple,
Ministry Begins,
Meets Nicodemus and the Samaritan.

Sermon on the Mount,
Jesus Feeds 5000,
Transfiguration, Miracles Abounding,
Parables, Triumphal Entry,
Olivet Discourse on Things to Be.

Last Passover, Crucifixion,
Resurrection, Ascension,
Pentecost, Holy Spirit Received,
Peter Preaches, 3000 Believe.

Stephen Martyred, Conversion of Saul,
Paul's First Journey, Jerusalem Council,
Paul's Second Journey, Thessalonians,
Romans, Galatians, Corinthians.

Paul Sent to Prison, Paul Stands Trial,
Paul Shipwrecked on an Isle,
Paul Writes More Letters from Prison,
Titus Sacks the Temple,
Revelation Vision.

Miracles of Jesus

The Lord turned water into wine,
Healed the sick, deaf, dumb and blind.

Cast out demons, calmed the sea,
Raised the dead, killed a tree.

Healed the lame, cured leprosy,
Restored a withered limb
and a severed ear,

Two enormous crowds He fed,
Walked on water, rose from the dead.

Hymns

The Old Rugged Cross
And Can It Be?
Be Still My Soul

Greek Alphabet

Αα	Ββ	Γγ	Δδ	Εε	Ζζ
Ηη	Θθ	Ιι	Κκ	Λλ	Μμ
Νν	Ξξ	Οο	Ππ	Ρρ	Σσς
Ττ	Υυ	Φφ	Χχ	Ψψ	Ωω

8
New Testament
MASTERY REVIEW
Cycle 8

Attributes of Yahweh

God's eternal, infinite,
Self-existent, self-sufficient,
God is omnipresent,
And omniscient.

God is immutable
Sovereign, wise, holy, good,
Righteous, just, faithful and true,
God is triune.

God is gracious, merciful,
He is spirit and life too,
God is omnipotent,
God is love, it's true!

John 1:1-14

In the beginning was the Word, and the
Word was with God, and the Word was
God. He was with God in the beginning.

Through Him all things were made;
without Him nothing was made that has
been made.

In Him was life, and that life was the light
of all mankind.

The light shines in the darkness, and the
darkness has not overcome it.

There was a man sent from God whose
name was John.

He came as a witness to testify
concerning that light, so that through him
all might believe.

He himself was not the light; he came
only as a witness to the light.

The true light that gives light to everyone
was coming into the world.

He was in the world, and though the
world was made through Him, the world
did not recognize Him.

He came to that which was His own, but
His own did not receive Him.

Yet to all who did receive Him, to those
who believed in His name, He gave the
right to become children of God—

children born not of natural descent, nor
of human decision or a husband's will, but
born of God.

The Word became flesh and made his
dwelling among us. We have seen His
glory, the glory of the one and only Son,
Who came from the Father, full of grace
and truth.

Churches of Revelation

Revelation churches are:
Ephesus, Smyrna, Pergamon,
Thyatira, Sardis, Philadelphia,
Laodicea, seven in all!

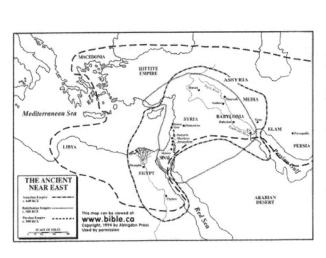

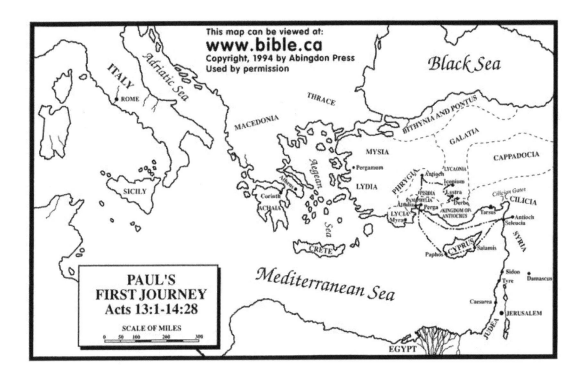

Classical
Sunday School

FAMILY DRILL BOOK
CYCLES 9 & 10

To learn more about Classical education, and for
great tips on using this Drill Book, go to
StrongHappyFamily.org.

BIBLE FACTS

Kings of Judah

To the tune of "Twinkle Twinkle"

Saul was Israel's first king,

He didn't please God in everything.

Next King David, Jesse's son,

Fought many battles,

And with God's help won.

The Temple was built by Solomon,

A very wise king and David's son.

TIMELINE

Creation

Fall

Cain and Abel

hymn

HE LEADETH ME
verse 1

He leadeth me:
O blessed thought!
O words with heavenly comfort fraught!
Whate'er I do, where'er I be,
still 'tis God's hand that leadeth me.

Refrain:
He leadeth me, He leadeth me;
by His own hand He leadeth me:
His faithful follower I would be,
for by His hand He leadeth me.

I PRACTICED:

☆ ☆ ☆ ☆ ☆ ☆

M	T	W	T	F	S
O	U	E	H	R	A
N	E	D	U	I	T

CYCLE 9

FALL

WEEK 1

GENESIS 1:1

In the beginning
God created
the heavens
and the earth.

related stories

Genesis 3

Vos Old
Testament
Lessons 5-7

Hurlbut Part 1
Lesson 1

Aleph
א

Bet
ב

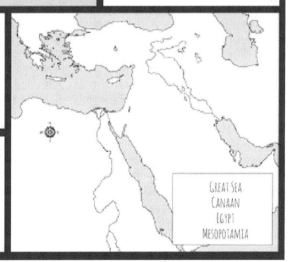

GREAT SEA
CANAAN
EGYPT
MESOPOTAMIA

BIBLE FACTS

Kings of Judah
To the tune of "Twinkle Twinkle"

With Rehoboam the kingdom split,

Egypt beat Judah and plundered it.

Abijah's rule was only three years long,

But he trusted God

And was make strong.

Then King Asa, wise and brave,

Beat his foes, cleared idols away.

TIMELINE

Flood

Job

Tower of Babel

hymn

HE LEADETH ME
verse 2

Sometimes mid scenes of deepest gloom,
sometimes where Eden's flowers bloom,
by waters calm, o'er troubled sea,
still 'tis God's hand that leadeth me.

He leadeth me, He leadeth me;
by His own hand He leadeth me:
His faithful follower I would be,
for by His hand He leadeth me.

I PRACTICED:

☆ ☆ ☆ ☆ ☆ ☆
M T W T F S
O U E H R A
N E D U I T

CYCLE 9

JOB

WEEK 2

GENESIS 1:2

Now the earth was formless and empty,

darkness was over the surface of the deep.

and the Spirit of God was hovering over the waters.

related stories

Job 1-42

Hurlbut Part 1 Lesson 35

Gimel
ג

Dalet
ד

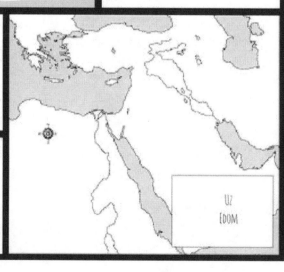

UZ
EDOM

BIBLE FACTS

Kings of Judah
To the tune of "Twinkle Twinkle"

While Judah was ruled by Jehoshaphat,

Israel's Ahab had his "at bat."

Together they fought the Syrians and won.

And Ahab's daughter married Big J's son.

Jehoshaphat's rule was biggest of all,

Used his power to make idols fall.

TIMELINE

Abraham

Ishmael

Sodom and Gomorrah

A	M	D	E
2000	1500	1000	500

hymn

HE LEADETH ME
verse 3

Lord, I would clasp Thy hand in mine,
nor ever murmur nor repine;
content, whatever lot I see,
since 'tis my God that leadeth me.

Refrain:
He leadeth me, He leadeth me;
by His own hand He leadeth me:
His faithful follower I would be,
for by His hand He leadeth me.

I PRACTICED:

☆ ☆ ☆ ☆ ☆

M	T	W	T	F	S
O	U	E	H	R	A
N	E	D	U	I	T

CYCLE 9

ISHMAEL

WEEK 3

Then God said, "Let Us make mankind in Our image, in Our likeness, so that they may rule over the fish in the sea and the birds in the sky, over the livestock and all the wild animals, and over all the creatures that move along the ground."

related stories

Genesis 16-17

Vos Old Testament Lessons 13, 15

Hurlbut Part 1 Lesson 9

He
ה

Vav
ו

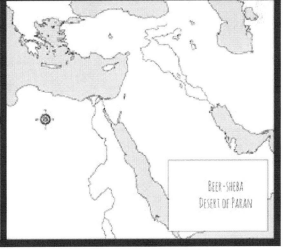

Beer-sheba
Desert of Paran

BIBLE FACTS

Kings of Judah

To the tune of "Twinkle Twinkle"

Jehoram to Athaliah was wed,

He worshiped idols, made his brothers dead.

Ahaziah ruled one year and was through,

He was murdered by the evil Jehu.

Athaliah gave herself the throne,

Killed her grandsons; made Baal a home.

TIMELINE

Isaac as well

Jacob and Esau

Israel's tribes

A	M	D	E
2000	1500	1000	500

hymn

HE LEADETH ME
verse 4

And when my task on earth is done,
when, by Thy grace, the victory's won,
e'en death's cold wave I will not flee,
since God through Jordan leadeth me.

Refrain:
He leadeth me, He leadeth me;
by His own hand He leadeth me:
His faithful follower I would be,
for by His hand He leadeth me.

I PRACTICED:

☆ ☆ ☆ ☆ ☆ ☆

M	T	W	T	F	S
O	U	E	H	R	A
N	E	D	U	I	T

CYCLE 9
JACOB AND ESAU
WEEK 4

GENESIS 1:27

So God created mankind in His own image, in the image of God He created them; male and female He created them.

related stories

Genesis 32

Vos Old Testament Lessons 18-20

Hurlbut Part 1 Lessons 12, 14

Zayin
ז

Het
ח

Sodom
Gomorrah
Dead Sea
Jordan River

BIBLE FACTS

Kings of Judah

To the Tune of "Twinkle Twinkle"

One baby grandson was hid away,

Six years in the Temple, night and day.

When Joash was presented by Jehoiada,

All the people ran and killed Athaliah.

While Jehoiada lived, Joash ruled well,

Then Joash sinned, to his servants fell.

TIMELINE

Joseph in Egypt

Moses' Life

Burning bush and plagues in Egypt

A	M	D	E
2000	1500	1000	500

hymn

STANDING ON THE PROMISES
verse 1

Standing on the promises of Christ my king,
through eternal ages let His praises ring;
glory in the highest, I will shout and sing,
standing on the promises of God.

Refrain:
Standing, standing,
standing on the promises of God my Savior;
standing, standing,
I'm standing on the promises of God.

I PRACTICED:

☆ ☆ ☆ ☆ ☆ ☆

M	T	W	T	F	S
O	U	E	H	R	A
N	E	D	U	I	T

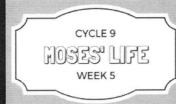

CYCLE 9
MOSES' LIFE
WEEK 5

GENESIS 1:28

God blessed them and said to them, "Be fruitful and increase in number; fill the earth and subdue it. Rule over the fish in the sea and the birds in the sky and over every living creature that moves on the ground."

related stories

Genesis
Exodus 2-40

Vos Old
Testament
Lesson 32

Hurlbut Part 1
Lessons 20, 34

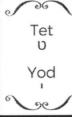

Tet
ט

Yod
י

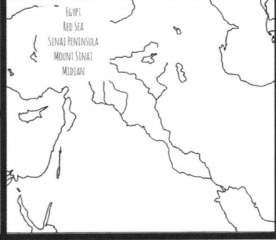

Egypt
Red Sea
Sinai Peninsula
Mount Sinai
Midian

BIBLE FACTS
Kings of Judah
To the tune of "Twinkle Twinkle"

Amaziah's rule started well,

But he worshiped idols, to his nobles fell.

Uzziah was strong and his kingdom grew,

But he wanted to be king and High Priest too.

As he stood before the altar in the Holy Place,

Incurable leprosy covered his face.

TIMELINE

Exodus and 10 Commandments

Desert, Ark, Feasts, Tabernacle

Joshua's Conquest

_A_	_M_	_D_	_E_
2000	1500	1000	500

hymn

STANDING ON THE PROMISES
verse 2

Standing on the promises that cannot fail,
when the howling storms of doubt and fear assail,
by the living Word of God I shall prevail,
standing on the promises of God.

Refrain:
Standing, standing,
standing on the promises of God my Savior;
standing, standing,
I'm standing on the promises of God.

I PRACTICED:

☆ ☆ ☆ ☆ ☆ ☆

M	T	W	T	F	S
O	U	E	H	R	A
N	E	D	U	I	T

CYCLE 9
DESERT, ARK, FEASTS, TABERNACLE
WEEK 6

GENESIS 1:29

Then God said, "I give you every seed-bearing plant on the face of the whole earth and every tree that has fruit with seed in it. They will be yours for food.

related stories

Exodus 16-40

Vos Old Testament Lessons 40-45

Hurlbut Part 1 Lessons 27-33

Kaf
כ
ך

Lamed
ל

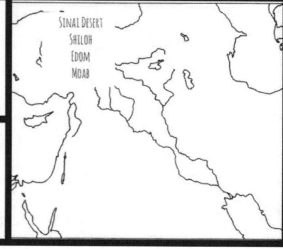

Sinai Desert
Shiloh
Edom
Moab

BIBLE FACTS

KINGS OF JUDAH

To the tune of "Twinkle Twinkle"

Jotham was upright, though his people would sin,

He worked on the Temple, but he never went in.

Ahaz, his son, was Judah's worst.

He sacrificed his sons, and his reign was cursed.

When his enemies beat him and he started to fail,

He didn't turn to God, he turned to Baal.

TIMELINE

Judges rule

Ruth and Boaz

King Saul's reign

A	M	D	E
2000	1500	1000	500

hymn

STANDING ON THE PROMISES
verse 3

Standing on the promises of Christ the Lord,
bound to Him eternally by love's strong cord,
overcoming daily with the Spirit's sword,
standing on the promises of God.

Refrain:
Standing, standing,
standing on the promises of God my Savior,
standing, standing,
I'm standing on the promises of God.

I PRACTICED:

☆ ☆ ☆ ☆ ☆

M	T	W	T	F	S
O	U	E	H	R	A
N	E	D	U	I	T

CYCLE 9
RUTH AND BOAZ
WEEK 7

GENESIS 1:30

And to all the beasts of the earth and all the birds in the sky and all the creatures that move along the ground —everything that has the breath of life in it—I give every green plant for food." And it was so.

related stories

Ruth 1-4

Vos Old Testament Lesson 64

Hurlbut Part 2 Lesson 14

Mem
ם
מ

BETHLEHEM
MOAB

BIBLE FACTS

Kings of Judah

To the tune of "Twinkle Twinkle"

While Assyria conquered the kingdom up north,

Hezekiah let Isaiah speak forth.

Hezekiah had a godly rule,

He was good and just and never cruel.

But his son Manasseh, for fifty years,

Reigned wickedly, left the people in tears.

TIMELINE

David's Kingdom

Psalms,
David's Covenant

Solomon's Temple,
Kingdom divides

A	M	D	E
2000	1500	1000	500

hymn

STANDING ON THE PROMISES
verse 4

Standing on the promises I cannot fall,
listening every moment to the Spirit's call,
resting in my Savior as my all in all,
standing on the promises of God

Refrain:
Standing, standing,
standing on the promises of God my
Savior,
standing, standing,
I'm standing on the promises of God.

I PRACTICED:

☆ ☆ ☆ ☆ ☆ ☆

M	T	W	T	F	S
O	U	E	H	R	A
N	E	D	U	I	T

CYCLE 9
PSALMS
DAVID'S COVENANT
WEEK 8

GENESIS 1:31

God saw all that He had made, and it was very good.

And there was evening, and there was morning —the sixth day.

related stories
Psalms 1-150
2 Samuel 7

Vos Old
Testament
Lessons 72-73

Hurlbut Part 3
Lessons 10, 11, 13

Nun

נ

ן

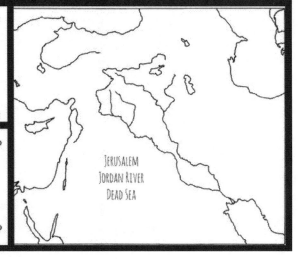

Jerusalem
Jordan River
Dead Sea

BIBLE FACTS

Kings of Judah

To the tune of "Twinkle Twinkle"

Ammon led two years, then met his fate.

Josiah took the throne when he was just eight.

He cleared away all the idols he saw.

He cleaned out the Temple

And discovered the Law.

King Jehoahaz was taken away,

In the land of Egypt he had to stay.

TIMELINE

Ahab and Elijah on the north side

Hezekiah and Isaiah in the South

Israel falls to Assyria's clout

A	M	D	E
2000	1500	1000	500

---

hymn

JUST AS I AM
verse 1

Just as I am,
without one plea,
but that Thy blood
was shed for me,
and that Thou bidd'st
me come to Thee,
O Lamb of God,
I come, I come.

I PRACTICED:

☆ ☆ ☆ ☆ ☆ ☆

M	T	W	T	F	S
O	U	E	H	R	A
N	E	D	U	I	T

CYCLE 9
HEZEKIAH AND ISAIAH
IN THE SOUTH
WEEK 9

GENESIS 2:1

Thus the heavens and the earth were completed in all their vast array.

---

related stories

Isaiah 1-66
2 Kings 18-20

Vos Old Testament Lessons 88, 90-93, 95-97

Hurlbut Part 5
Lessons 1-5

Samekh
ס
Ayin
ע

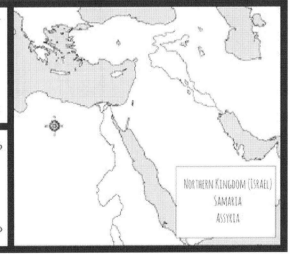

Northern Kingdom (Israel)
Samaria
Assyria

BIBLE FACTS

Kings of Judah

To the tune of "Twinkle Twinkle"

Hezekiah's other son took the throne.

Jehoiakin's evil became well-known.

He tried to kill the prophet Jeremiah.

And died in a prison in Babylonia.

Jehoichin and Zedekiah, the last,

In Babylon's jail their last days passed.

TIMELINE

Jeremiah and Ezekiel warn Judah

Judah falls to Babylon, Temple ruined

Daniel in the Exile

A_____M_____D____E__
2000   1500   1000   500

hymn

JUST AS I AM
verse 2

Just as I am, and waiting not

to rid my soul of one dark blot,

to Thee, Whose blood

can cleanse each spot,

O Lamb of God, I come, I come.

I PRACTICED:

☆ ☆ ☆ ☆ ☆ ☆

M	T	W	T	F	S
O	U	E	H	R	A
N	E	D	U	I	T

CYCLE 9
JUDAH FALLS TO BABYLON
TEMPLE RUINED
WEEK 10

GENESIS 2:2

By the seventh day God had finished the work He had been doing; so on the seventh day He rested from all His work.

related stories

2 Chronicles 36

Vos Old Testament Lessons 98-99

Hurlbut Part 5 Lessons 6-7

Pe
פ
ף
Tsadi
צ
ץ

SOUTHERN KINGDOM (JUDAH)
BABYLON

BIBLE FACTS

Kings of Judah

To the tune of "Twinkle Twinkle"

Still in David's royal line,

Sits the mighty King Divine.

Born into a manger lowly,

Died to make His people holy.

All who in Jesus believe,

Will eternal life receive.

TIMELINE

Cyrus' decree
Exiles return

Temple rebuilding

Esther saves the Jews

A	M	D	E
2000	1500	1000	500

hymn

JUST AS I AM
verse 3

Just as I am,
though tossed about
with many a conflict,
many a doubt,
fightings and fears
within, without,
O Lamb of God,
I come, I come.

I PRACTICED:

☆ ☆ ☆ ☆ ☆ ☆

M	T	W	T	F	S
O	U	E	H	R	A
N	E	D	U	I	T

CYCLE 9

TEMPLE REBUILDING

WEEK 11

GENESIS 2:3

Then God blessed the seventh day and made it holy, because on it He rested from all the work of creating that He had done.

related stories

Haggai 1-2

Vos Old Testament Lesson 109

Hurlbut Part 5 Lesson 14

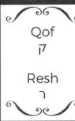

Qof
ק

Resh
ר

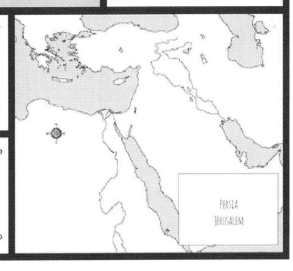

Persia
Jerusalem

BIBLE FACTS

Kings of Judah

To the tune of "Twinkle Twinkle"

REVIEW!

Nehemiah builds the wall

Malachi foretells John the Baptist's call

Maccabean period ends here, no word from God for 400 years

A	M	D	E
2000	1500	1000	500

hymn

JUST AS I AM
verse 4

Just as I am,
Thou wilt receive,
wilt welcome, pardon,
cleanse, relieve;
because Thy promise
I believe,
O Lamb of God,
I come, I come.

I PRACTICED:

☆ ☆ ☆ ☆ ☆ ☆

M	T	W	T	F	S
O	U	E	H	R	A
N	E	D	U	I	T

CYCLE 9
MALACHI
WEEK 12

GENESIS 1:1–2, 26–2:3

REVIEW!

related stories

Malachi 3-4

Vos
New Testament
Lesson 1

Hurlbut Part 5
Lesson 18

Shin
ש

Tav
ת

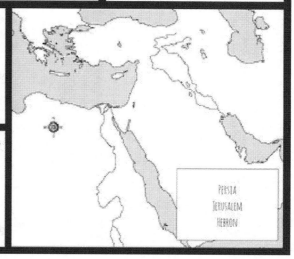

PERSIA
JERUSALEM
HEBRON

BIBLE FACTS
Catechism Q.1

Q. What is the chief end of man?

A. Man's chief end is to glorify God, and to enjoy him forever.

TIMELINE

John the Baptist

Messiah is born

Shepherds and Magi visit the Lord

J	R	P	T	R
-5	33	46-58	70	96

hymn
NOW THANK WE ALL OUR GOD
verse 1

Now thank we all our God
with heart and hands and voices,
Who wondrous things has done,
in Whom His world rejoices;
Who from our mothers' arms
has blessed us on our way
with countless gifts of love,
and still is ours today.

I PRACTICED:
☆ ☆ ☆ ☆ ☆
M	T	W	T	F	S
O	U	E	H	R	A
N	E	D	U	I	T

CYCLE 10
MESSIAH IS BORN
WEEK 1

MATTHEW 5:3-4

Blessed are the
poor in spirit,
for theirs is the
kingdom of heaven.

Blessed are those
who mourn,
for they will be
comforted.

related stories

Luke 2

Vos New
Testament
Lessons 2-4

Hurlbut Part 6
Lesson 2

Alpha
A α

Beta
B β

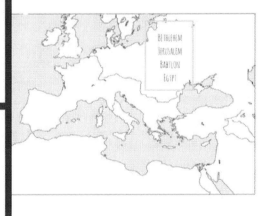

BIBLE FACTS
CATECHISM Q.2

Q. What rule has God given to direct us how we may glorify and enjoy Him?

A. The word of God, namely the Scriptures of the Old and New Testaments, is the only rule to direct us how we may glorify and enjoy Him.

TIMELINE

Flight into Egypt
Herod's Slaughter

Boy Jesus at the Temple

Baptism at the Jordan

J	R	P	T	R
-5	33	46-58	70	96

hymn

NOW THANK WE ALL OUR GOD
verse 2

O may this bounteous God

through all our life be near us,

with ever joyful hearts

and blessed peace to cheer us,

to keep us in His grace,

and guide us when perplexed,

and free us from all ills

of this world in the next.

I PRACTICED:

☆ ☆ ☆ ☆ ☆ ☆

M	T	W	T	F	S
O	U	E	H	R	A
N	E	D	U	I	T

CYCLE 10
BOY JESUS
AT THE TEMPLE
WEEK 2

MATTHEW 5:5-6

Blessed are the meek,
for they will inherit
the earth.

Blessed are those who
hunger and thirst for
righteousness,
for they will be filled.

related stories

Luke 2

Vos New
Testament
Lesson 6

Hurlbut Part 6
Lesson 4

Gamma
Γ γ

Delta
Δ δ

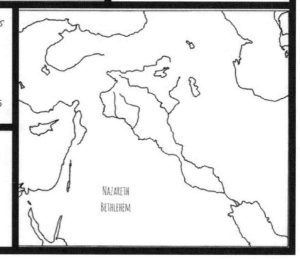

NAZARETH
BETHLEHEM

BIBLE FACTS

Catechism Q.3

Q. Are the Scriptures trustworthy in all that they affirm?

A. The Scriptures of both the Old and New Testaments, being Godbreathed, are infallible and inerrant in all their parts and are, therefore, trustworthy in all that they affirm concerning history, science, doctrine, ethics, religious practice, or any other topic.

TIMELINE

Temptation in the desert

Disciples' Call

Cana Wedding
Jubilee Inaugural

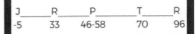

J	R	P	T	R
-5	33	46-58	70	96

hymn

NOW THANK WE ALL OUR GOD
verse 3

All praise and thanks to God
the Father now be given,
the Son and Spirit blest,
Who reign in highest heaven
the one eternal God,
Whom heaven and earth adore;
for thus it was, is now,
and shall be evermore.

I PRACTICED:

☆ ☆ ☆ ☆ ☆

M	T	W	T	F	S
O	U	E	H	R	A
N	E	D	U	I	T

CYCLE 10

DISCIPLES' CALL

WEEK 3

MATTHEW 5:7-8

Blessed are the merciful,
for they
will be shown mercy.

Blessed are the pure in heart,
for they will see God.

related stories

Matthew 4
Mark 1

Vos New
Testament
Lesson 8

Hurlbut Part 6
Lesson 6, 13

Epsilon
E ε

Zeta
Z ζ

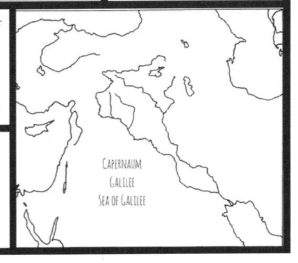

Capernaum
Galilee
Sea of Galilee

BIBLE FACTS
CATECHISM Q.4

Q. What do the Scriptures principally teach?

A. The Scriptures principally teach what man is to believe concerning God, and what duty God requires of man.

TIMELINE

Jesus clears the Temple, Ministry begins

Meets Nicodemus and the Samaritan

Sermon on the Mount

J	R	P	T	R
-5	33	46-58	70	96

hymn

TAKE MY LIFE
verse 1

Take my life and let it be
consecrated, Lord, to Thee.
Take my moments
and my days;
let them flow
in endless praise,
let them flow
in endless praise.

I PRACTICED:

☆ ☆ ☆ ☆ ☆ ☆

M	T	W	T	F	S
O	U	E	H	R	A
N	E	D	U	I	T

CYCLE 10
JESUS MEETS NICODEMUS AND THE SAMARITAN WOMAN
WEEK 4

MATTHEW 5:9–10

Blessed are the peacemakers,
for they will be called children of God.

Blessed are those who are persecuted because of righteousness,
for theirs is the kingdom of heaven.

related stories

John 3-4

Vos New Testament Lessons 12, 13

Hurlbut Part 6 Lesson 8

Eta
H η

Theta
Θ θ

SAMARIA
JERUSALEM

BIBLE FACTS

CATECHISM Q. 5

Q. What is God?

A. God is a Spirit, infinite, eternal, and unchangeable, in His being, wisdom, power, holiness, justice, goodness, and truth.

Jesus feeds 5000, Transfiguration, Miracles abounding

J	R	P	T	R
-5	33	46-58	70	96

hymn

TAKE MY LIFE
verse 2

Take my hands
and let them move
at the impulse of Thy love.
Take my feet
and let them be
swift and beautiful for Thee,
swift and beautiful for Thee.

I PRACTICED:

☆ ☆ ☆ ☆ ☆ ☆

M	T	W	T	F	S
O	U	E	H	R	A
N	E	D	U	I	T

CYCLE 10
TRANSFIGURATION
WEEK 5

MATTHEW 5:11-12

Blessed are you when people insult you, persecute you and falsely say all kinds of evil against you because of Me.

Rejoice and be glad, because great is your reward in heaven, for in the same way they persecuted the prophets who were before you.

related stories

Matthew 17,
Luke 9

Vos New
Testament
Lessons 31, 32

Hurlbut Part 6
Lesson 21

Iota
I ι

Kappa
K κ

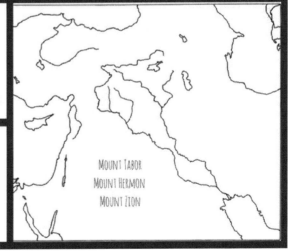

Mount Tabor
Mount Hermon
Mount Zion

BIBLE FACTS
Catechism Q. 6

Q. Are there more Gods than one?

A. There is but one only, the living and true God.

TIMELINE

Parables

Triumphal Entry

Olivet Discourse on

things to be

J	R	P	T	R
-5	33	46-58	70	96

hymn

TAKE MY LIFE
verse 3

Take my voice
and let me sing
always, only,
for my King.
Take my lips
and let them be
filled with messages
from Thee,
filled with messages
from Thee.

I PRACTICED:
☆ ☆ ☆ ☆ ☆ ☆
M T W T F S
O U E H R A
N E D U I T

CYCLE 10
TRIUMPHAL ENTRY
WEEK 6

MATTHEW 5:13-14

You are the salt of the earth. But if the salt loses its saltiness, how can it be made salty again? It is no longer good for anything, except to be thrown out and trampled underfoot.

You are the light of the world. A town built on a hill cannot be hidden.

related stories
Mark 11
Matthew 21

Vos New
Testament
Lesson 41

Hurlbut Part 6
Lesson 30

Lambda
Λ λ

Mu
M μ

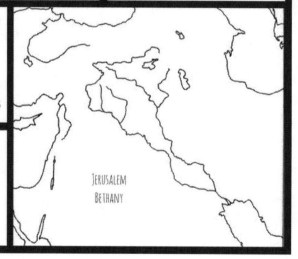
Jerusalem
Bethany

BIBLE FACTS

Catechism Q. 7

Q. How many persons are there in the Godhead?

A. There are three persons in the Godhead: the Father, the Son, and the Holy Spirit; and these three are one God, the same in substance, equal in power and glory.

TIMELINE

Last Passover

Crucifixion

Resurrection

J	R	P	T	R
-5	33	46-58	70	96

hymn

TAKE MY LIFE
verse 4

Take my silver and my gold;
not a mite
would I withhold.
Take my intellect and use
every power
as Thou shalt choose,
every power
as Thou shalt choose.

I PRACTICED:

☆ ☆ ☆ ☆ ☆ ☆

M	T	W	T	F	S
O	U	E	H	R	A
N	E	D	U	I	T

CYCLE 10
CRUCIFIXION
WEEK 7

MATTHEW 5:15-16

Neither do people light a lamp and put it under a bowl. Instead they put it on its stand, and it gives light to everyone in the house.

In the same way, let your light shine before others, that they may see your good deeds and glorify your Father in heaven.

related stories

Matthew 27,
Luke 23, John 19

Vos New
Testament
Lessons 46-51

Hurlbut Part 6
Lessons 35, 36

Nu
N ν

Xi
Ξ ξ

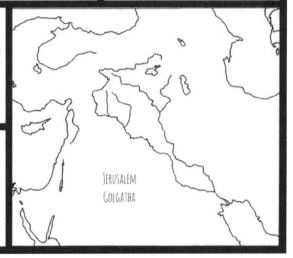

Jerusalem
Golgatha

BIBLE FACTS
Catechism Q. 9

Q. How does God execute His decrees?

A. God executes His decrees in the works of creation and providence.

Ascension

Pentecost, Holy Spirit received

Peter preaches, 3,000 believe

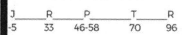

J	R	P	T	R
-5	33	46-58	70	96

hymn

TAKE MY LIFE
verse 5

Take my will
and make it Thine;
it shall be no longer mine.
Take my heart
it is Thine own;
it shall be Thy royal throne,
it shall be Thy royal throne.

I PRACTICED:
☆ ☆ ☆ ☆ ☆ ☆

M	T	W	T	F	S
O	U	E	H	R	A
N	E	D	U	I	T

CYCLE 10
PENTECOST
WEEK 8

MATTHEW 5:17

Do not think that I have come to abolish the Law or the Prophets;

I have not come to abolish them but to fulfill them.

related stories

Acts 2

Vos New Testament Lessons 57

Hurlbut Part 7 Lesson 1

Omicron
O o

Pi
Π π

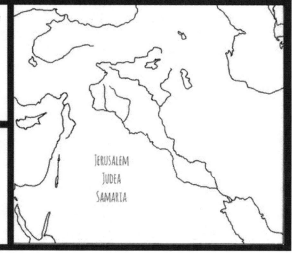

Jerusalem
Judea
Samaria

BIBLE FACTS
CATECHISM Q. 10

Q. What is the work of creation?

A. The work of creation is God's making all things of nothing, by the word of His power, in the space of six days, and all very good.

TIMELINE

Stephen martyred

Conversion of Saul

Paul's first journey

J	R	P	T	R
-5	33	46-58	70	96

hymn

TAKE MY LIFE
verse 6

Take my love; my Lord, I pour

at Thy feet its treasure store.

Take myself, and I will be

ever, only, all for Thee,

ever, only, all for Thee.

I PRACTICED:
☆ ☆ ☆ ☆ ☆ ☆

M	T	W	T	F	S
O	U	E	H	R	A
N	E	D	U	I	T

CYCLE 10
CONVERSION OF SAUL
WEEK 9

MATTHEW 5:18

For truly I tell you, until heaven and earth disappear, not the smallest letter, not the least stroke of a pen, will by any means disappear from the Law until everything is accomplished.

related stories

Acts 9

Vos New Testament Lessons 64-66

Hurlbut Part 7 Lesson 6

Rho
P ρ

Sigma
Σ σ

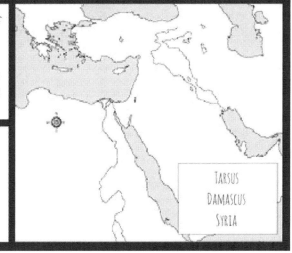

Tarsus
Damascus
Syria

BIBLE FACTS

CATECHISM Q. 11

Q. How did God create man?

A. God created man, male and female, after His own image, in knowledge, righteousness, and holiness, with dominion over the creatures.

TIMELINE

Jerusalem Council

Paul's Second Journey

Thessalonians, Galatians, Romans, Corinthians

J	R	P	T	R
-5	33	46-58	70	96

hymn

I KNOW NOT WHY GOD'S WONDROUS GRACE
verse 1

I know not why God's wondrous grace
To me He hath made known,
Nor why, unworthy, Christ in love
Redeemed me for His own.

Refrain:
But "I know Whom I have believed,
And am persuaded that He is able
To keep that which I've committed
Unto Him against that day."

I PRACTICED:

☆ ☆ ☆ ☆ ☆ ☆

M	T	W	T	F	S
O	U	E	H	R	A
N	E	D	U	I	T

CYCLE 10
PAUL'S 2nd JOURNEY
WEEK 10

MATTHEW 5:19

Therefore anyone who sets aside one of the least of these commands and teaches others accordingly will be called least in the kingdom of heaven, but whoever practices and teaches these commands will be called great in the kingdom of heaven.

related stories

Acts 15-18

Vos New Testament Lessons 71-80

Hurlbut Part 7 Lessons 10-14

Tau
Τ τ

Upsilon
Υ υ

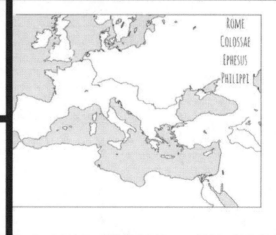

ROME
COLOSSAE
EPHESUS
PHILIPPI

BIBLE FACTS

CATECHISM REVEIW, Q. 1-5

Q. 1 What is the chief end of man?

A. 1 Man's chief end is to glorify God, and to enjoy Him forever.

Q. 2 What rule has God given to direct us how we may glorify and enjoy Him?

A. 2 The word of God, namely the Scriptures of the Old and New Testaments, is the only rule to direct us how we may glorify and enjoy Him.

Q. 3 Are the Scriptures trustworthy in all that they affirm?

A. 3 The Scriptures of both the Old and New Testaments, being Godbreathed, are infallible and inerrant in all their parts and are, therefore, trustworthy in all that they affirm concerning history, science, doctrine, ethics, religious practice, or any other topic.

Q. 4 What do the Scriptures principally teach?

A. 4 The Scriptures principally teach what man is to believe concerning God, and what duty God requires of man.

Q. 5 What is God?

A. 5 God is a Spirit, infinite, eternal, and unchangeable, in His being, wisdom, power, holiness, justice, goodness, and truth.

TIMELINE

Paul sent to prison

Paul stands trial

Paul shipwrecked on an isle

J	R	P	T	R
-5	33	46-58	70	96

hymn

I KNOW NOT WHY GOD'S WONDROUS GRACE
verse 2

I know not how this saving faith
To me He did impart,
Nor how believing in His Word
Wrought peace within my heart.

Refrain:
But "I know Whom I have believed,
And am persuaded that He is able
To keep that which I've committed
Unto Him against that day."

I PRACTICED:

☆ ☆ ☆ ☆ ☆ ☆

M	T	W	T	F	S
O	U	E	H	R	A
N	E	D	U	I	T

CYCLE 10

PAUL STANDS TRIAL

WEEK 11

MATTHEW 5:20

For I tell you that unless your righteousness surpasses that of the Pharisees and the teachers of the law, you will certainly not enter the kingdom of heaven.

related stories

Acts 22-26

Vos New Testament Lessons 81-87

Hurlbut Part 7 Lesson 15, 19

Phi
Φ φ

Chi
Χ χ

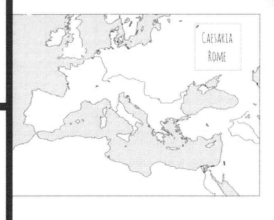

CAESARIA
ROME

BIBLE FACTS

Catechism Q. 6-7, 9-11 Review

Q. 6 Are there more Gods than one?
A. 6 There is but one only, the living and true God.

Q. 7 How many persons are there in the Godhead?
A. 7 There are three persons in the Godhead: the Father, the Son, and the Holy Spirit; and these three are one God, the same in substance, equal in power and glory.

Q. 9 How does God execute His decrees?
A. 9 God executes His decrees in the works of creation and providence.

Q. 10 What is the work of creation?
A. 10 The work of creation is God's making all things of nothing, by the word of His power, in the space of six days, and all very good.

Q. 11 How did God create man?
A. 11 God created man, male and female, after His own image, in knowledge, righteousness, and holiness, with dominion over the creatures.

TIMELINE

Paul writes more letters from prison

Titus sacks the Temple

Revelation vision

J	R	P		T	R
-5	33	46-58		70	96

hymn

I KNOW NOT WHY GOD'S WONDROUS GRACE
verse 3

I know not how the Spirit moves,
Convincing men of sin,
Revealing Jesus through the Word,
Creating faith in Him.

Refrain:
But "I know Whom I have believed,
And am persuaded that He is able
To keep that which I've committed
Unto Him against that day."

I PRACTICED:

☆ ☆ ☆ ☆ ☆ ☆

M	T	W	T	F	S
O	U	E	H	R	A
N	E	D	U	I	T

CYCLE 10

TITUS SACKS THE TEMPLE

WEEK 12

MATTHEW 5:3-20

REVIEW!

related stories

Matthew 24
Luke 21

Psi
Ψ ψ

Omega
Ω ω

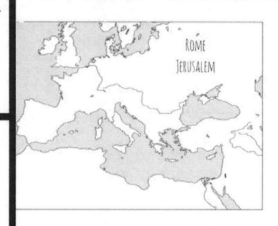

ROME

Jerusalem

Old Testament Timeline

Creation, Fall, Cain and Abel,
Flood, Job, Tower of Babel,
Abraham, Ishmael,
Sodom and Gomorrah, Isaac as Well.

Jacob and Esau, Israel's Tribes,
Joseph in Egypt, Moses' Life,
Burning Bush and Plagues in Egypt,
Exodus and Ten Commandments.

Desert, Ark, Feasts, Tabernacle,
Joshua's Conquest, Judges Rule,
Ruth and Boaz, King Saul's Reign, David's
Kingdom, Psalms, David's Covenant.

Solomon's Temple, Kingdom Divides,
Ahab and Elijah on the North Side, Hezekiah
and Isaiah in the South,
Israel Falls to Assyria's Clout.

Jeremiah and Ezekiel Warn Judah,
Judah Falls To Babylon,
Temple Ruined,
Daniel in the Exile, Cyrus' Decree,
Exiles Return, Temple Rebuilding.

Esther Saves the Jews,
Nehemiah Builds the Wall,
Malachi Foretells John the Baptist's Call,
Maccabean Period Ends Here,
No Word from God for 400 Years.

Hebrew Alphabet

Hymns

He Leadeth Me
Standing on the Promises of God
Just As I Am

9
Old Testament
MASTERY REVIEW
Cycle 9

Genesis 1:1-2, 1:26-2:3

In the beginning God created the heavens and the earth.

Now the earth was formless and empty, darkness was over the surface of the deep, and the Spirit of God was hovering over the waters. Then God said, "Let us make mankind in our image, in our likeness, so that they may rule over the fish in the sea and the birds in the sky, over the livestock and all the wild animals, and over all the creatures that move along the ground."

So God created mankind in his own image, in the image of God he created them; male and female he created them.

God blessed them and said to them, "Be fruitful and increase in number; fill the earth and subdue it. Rule over the fish in the sea and the birds in the sky and over every living creature that moves on the ground."

Then God said, "I give you every seed-bearing plant on the face of the whole earth and every tree that has fruit with seed in it. They will be yours for food.

And to all the beasts of the earth and all the birds in the sky and all the creatures that move along the ground —everything that has the breath of life in it—I give every green plant for food." And it was so.

God saw all that he had made, and it was very good. And there was evening, and there was morning—the sixth day.

Thus the heavens and the earth were completed in all their vast array.

By the seventh day God had finished the work he had been doing; so on the seventh day he rested from all his work.

Then God blessed the seventh day and made it holy, because on it he rested from all the work of creating that he had done.

Kings of Judah

Saul was Israel's first king. He didn't please God in everything. Next King David, Jesse's son, Fought many battles, and with God's help won. The Temple was built by Solomon. A very wise king and David's son.

With Rehoboam the kingdom split, Egypt beat Judah and plundered it. Abijah's rule was only three years long, But he trusted God and was make strong. Then King Asa, wise and brave, Beat his foes, cleared idols away.

While Judah was ruled by Jehoshaphat, Israel's Ahab had his "at bat." Together they fought the Syrians and won. And Ahab's daughter married Big J's son. Jehoshaphat's rule was biggest of all, Used his power to make idols fall.

Jehoram to Athaliah was wed, He worshiped idols, made his brothers dead. Ahaziah ruled one year and was through, He was murdered by the evil Jehu. Athaliah gave herself the throne. Killed her grandsons; made Baal a home.

One baby grandson was hid away, Six years in the Temple, night and day. When Joash was presented by Jehoiada, All the people ran and killed Athaliah. While Jehoiada lived, Joash ruled well, Then Joash sinned, to his servants fell.

Amaziah's rule started well, But he worshiped idols, to his nobles fell. Uzziah was strong and his kingdom grew, But he wanted to be king and High Priest too. As he stood before the altar in the Holy Place, Incurable leprosy covered his face.

Jotham was upright though his people would sin, He worked on the Temple, but he never went in. Ahaz, his son, was Judah's worst. He sacrificed his sons, and his reign was cursed. When his enemies beat him and he started to fail, He didn't turn to God, he turned to Baal.

While Assyria conquered the kingdom up north, Hezekiah let Isaiah speak forth. Hezekiah had a godly rule. He was good and just and never cruel. But his son Manasseh, for fifty years, Reigned wickedly, left the people in tears.

Ammon led two years, then met his fate. Josiah took the throne when he was just eight. He cleared away all the idols he saw. He cleaned out the Temple and discovered the Law. King Jehoahaz was taken away, In the land of Egypt he had to stay.

Hezekiah's other son took the throne. Jehoiakin's evil became well-known. He tried to kill the prophet Jeremiah. And died in a prison in Babylonia. Jehoichin and Zedekiah, the last, In Babylon's jail their last days passed.

Still in David's royal line, Sits the mighty King Divine. Born into a manger lowly, Died to make His people holy. All who in Jesus believe, Will eternal life receive.

New Testament Timeline

John the Baptist, Messiah Is Born,
Shepherds and Magi Visit the Lord,
Flight into Egypt, Herod's Slaughter,
Boy Jesus at the Temple,
Baptism at the Jordan.

Temptation in the Desert,
Disciples' Call, Cana Wedding,
Jubilee Inaugural
Jesus Clears the Temple,
Ministry Begins,
Meets Nicodemus and the Samaritan.

Sermon on the Mount,
Jesus Feeds 5000,
Transfiguration, Miracles Abounding,
Parables, Triumphal Entry,
Olivet Discourse on Things to Be.

Last Passover, Crucifixion,
Resurrection, Ascension,
Pentecost, Holy Spirit Received,
Peter Preaches, 3000 Believe.

Stephen Martyred, Conversion of Saul,
Paul's First Journey, Jerusalem Council,
Paul's Second Journey, Thessalonians,
Romans, Galatians, Corinthians.

Paul Sent to Prison, Paul Stands Trial,
Paul Shipwrecked on an Isle,
Paul Writes More Letters from Prison,
Titus Sacks the Temple,
Revelation Vision.

Greek Alphabet

GREEK ALPHABET

Αα	Ββ	Γγ	Δδ	Εε	Ζζ
Ηη	Θθ	Ιι	Κκ	Λλ	Μμ
Νν	Ξξ	Οο	Ππ	Ρρ	Σσς
Ττ	Υυ	Φφ	Χχ	Ψψ	Ωω

Hymns

Now Thank We All Our God
Take My Life
I Know Not Why God's Wondrous Love

Catechism

Q. 1 What is the chief end of man?

A. 1 Man's chief end is to glorify God, and to enjoy Him forever.

Q. 2 What rule has God given to direct us how we may glorify and enjoy Him?

A. 2 The word of God, namely the Scriptures of the Old and New Testaments, is the only rule to direct us how we may glorify and enjoy Him.

Q. 3 Are the Scriptures trustworthy in all that they affirm?

A. 3 The Scriptures of both the Old and New Testaments, being Godbreathed, are infallible and inerrant in all their parts and are, therefore, trustworthy in all that they affirm concerning history, science, doctrine, ethics, religious practice, or any other topic.

Q. 4 What do the Scriptures principally teach?

A. 4 The Scriptures principally teach what man is to believe concerning God, and what duty God requires of man.

Q. 5 What is God?

A. 5 God is a Spirit, infinite, eternal, and unchangeable, in His being, wisdom, power, holiness, justice, goodness, and truth.

Q. 6 Are there more Gods than one?

A. 6 There is but one only, the living and true God.

Q. 7 How many persons are there in the Godhead?

A. 7 There are three persons in the Godhead: the Father, the Son, and the Holy Spirit; and these three are one God, the same in substance, equal in power and glory.

Q. 9 How does God execute His decrees?

A. 9 God executes His decrees in the works of creation and providence.

Q. 10 What is the work of creation?

A. 10 The work of creation is God's making all things of nothing, by the word of His power, in the space of six days, and all very good.

Q. 11 How did God create man?

A. 11 God created man, male and female, after His own image, in knowledge, righteousness, and holiness, with dominion over the creatures.

Matthew 5:3-20

Blessed are the poor in spirit,
  for theirs is the kingdom of heaven.
Blessed are those who mourn,
  for they will be comforted.
Blessed are the meek,
  for they will inherit the earth.
Blessed are those who hunger and
  thirst for righteousness, for they will
  be filled.
Blessed are the merciful,
  for they will be shown mercy.
Blessed are the pure in heart,
  for they will see God.
Blessed are the peacemakers,
  for they will be called children of God.
Blessed are those who are persecuted
  because of righteousness, for theirs is
  the kingdom of heaven.

Blessed are you when people insult you, persecute you and falsely say all kinds of evil against you because of Me. Rejoice and be glad, because great is your reward in heaven, for in the same way they persecuted the prophets who were before you. You are the salt of the earth. But if the salt loses its saltiness, how can it be made salty again? It is no longer good for anything, except to be thrown out and trampled underfoot. You are the light of the world. A town built on a hill cannot be hidden. Neither do people light a lamp and put it under a bowl. Instead they put it on its stand, and it gives light to everyone in the house. In the same way, let your light shine before others, that they may see your good deeds and glorify your Father in heaven. Do not think that I have come to abolish the Law or the Prophets; I have not come to abolish them but to fulfill them. For truly I tell you, until heaven and earth disappear, not the smallest letter, not the least stroke of a pen, will by any means disappear from the Law until everything is accomplished. Therefore anyone who sets aside one of the least of these commands and teaches others accordingly will be called least in the kingdom of heaven, but whoever practices and teaches these commands will be called great in the kingdom of heaven. For I tell you that unless your righteousness surpasses that of the Pharisees and the teachers of the law, you will certainly not enter the kingdom of heaven.

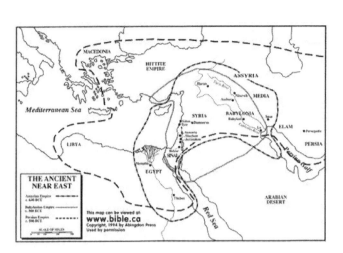

THE ANCIENT
NEAR EAST

Israel
at the
Time of Christ
30 AD

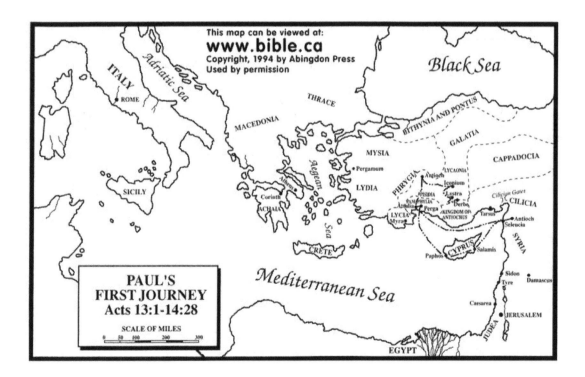

PAUL'S
FIRST JOURNEY
Acts 13:1-14:28

SCALE OF MILES

Classical
Sunday School

FAMILY DRILL BOOK
CYCLES 11 & 12

To learn more about Classical education, and for
great tips on using this Drill Book, go to
StrongHappyFamily.org

BIBLE FACTS

Hebrew Religious Calendar
To the tune of "Nobody Likes Me"

Nisan, Iyar, Sivan, Tammuz

Av, Elul, Tishri, Heshvan

Kislev, Teveth, Shevat, Adar,

and Adar Bet!

TIMELINE

Creation

Fall

Cain and Abel

hymn

JOYFUL, JOYFUL
verse 1

Joyful, joyful, we adore You,
God of glory, Lord of love;
Hearts unfold like flow'rs
before You,
Op'ning to the sun above.
Melt the clouds of sin and
sadness;
Drive the dark of doubt
away;
Giver of immortal gladness,
Fill us with the light of day!

I PRACTICED:

☆ ☆ ☆ ☆ ☆ ☆

M	T	W	T	F	S
O	U	E	H	R	A
N	E	D	U	I	T

CYCLE 11
CAIN AND ABEL
WEEK 1

PROVERBS 3:1

My son, do not forget
my teaching,

but keep my
commands
in your heart,

related stories
Genesis 4

Vos Old
Testament
Lessons 8-9

Hurlbut Part 1
Lesson 2

Hear
שְׁמַע
Shema

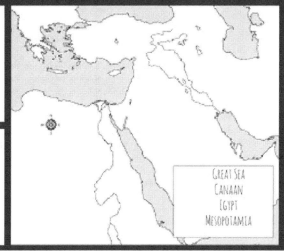

GREAT SEA
CANAAN
EGYPT
MESOPOTAMIA

BIBLE FACTS

Hebrew Religious Calendar
To the tune of "Nobody Likes Me"

Nisan, Iyar, Sivan, Tammuz

Av, Elul, Tishri, Heshvan

Kislev, Teveth, Shevat, Adar,

and Adar Bet!

TIMELINE

Flood

Job

Tower of Babel

hymn

JOYFUL, JOYFUL
verse 2
All Your works
with joy surround You,
Earth and heav'n reflect Your rays,
Stars and angels sing around You,
Center of unbroken praise;
Field and forest,
vale and mountain,
Flow'ry meadow, flashing sea,
Chanting bird
and flowing fountain
Praising You eternally!

I PRACTICED:
☆ ☆ ☆ ☆ ☆ ☆

M	T	W	T	F	S
O	U	E	H	R	A
N	E	D	U	I	T

CYCLE 11
TOWER OF BABEL
WEEK 2

PROVERBS 3:2

for they will prolong
your life many years

and bring you peace
and prosperity.

related stories
Genesis 11

Vos Old
Testament
Lesson 11

Hurlbut Part 1
Lesson 4

O Israel
יִשְׂרָאֵל.
Yisrael

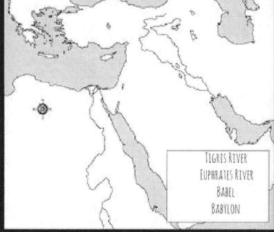

Tigris River
Euphrates River
Babel
Babylon

BIBLE FACTS

HEBREW RELIGIOUS CALENDAR
To the tune of "Nobody Likes Me"

Nisan, Iyar, Sivan, Tammuz

Av, Elul, Tishri, Heshvan

Kislev, Teveth, Shevat, Adar,

and Adar Bet!

TIMELINE

Abraham

Ishmael

Sodom and Gomorrah

A	M	D	E
2000	1500	1000	500

hymn

JOYFUL, JOYFUL
verse 3

Always giving and forgiving,
Ever blessing, ever blest,
Well-spring of the joy of living,
Ocean-depth of happy rest!
Loving Father,
Christ our Brother,
Let Your light upon us shine:
Teach us how
to love each other,
Lift us to the joy divine.

I PRACTICED:
☆ ☆ ☆ ☆ ☆ ☆
M	T	W	T	F	S
O	U	E	H	R	A
N	E	D	U	I	T

CYCLE 11

SODOM AND GOMORRAH

WEEK 3

PROVERBS 3:3

Let love and faithfulness
never leave you;

bind them
around your neck,
write them on the
tablet of your heart.

related stories

Genesis 18-19

Vos Old
Testament
Lesson 14

Hurlbut Part 1
Lesson 6-8

Yahweh
יהוה
Yahweh

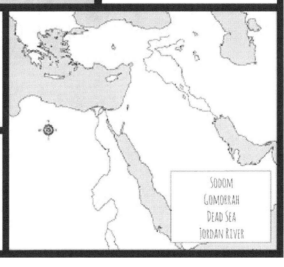

Sodom
Gomorrah
Dead Sea
Jordan River

BIBLE FACTS

Hebrew Religious Calendar
To the tune of "Nobody Likes Me"

Nisan, Iyar, Sivan, Tammuz

Av, Elul, Tishri, Heshvan

Kislev, Teveth, Shevat, Adar,

and Adar Bet!

TIMELINE

Isaac as well

Jacob and Esau

Israel's tribes

A	M	D	E
2000	1500	1000	500

hymn

JOYFUL JOYFUL
verse 4

Mortals, join the mighty chorus,
Which the morning stars began;
God's own love is reigning o'er us,
Joining people hand in hand.
Ever singing, march we onward,
Victors in the midst of strife;
Joyful music leads us sunward
In the triumph song of life.

I PRACTICED:
☆ ☆ ☆ ☆ ☆ ☆

M	T	W	T	F	S
O	U	E	H	R	A
N	E	D	U	I	T

CYCLE 11
ISRAEL'S TRIBES
WEEK 4

PROVERBS 3:4

Then you
will win favor
and a good name

in the sight of
God and man.

related stories

Genesis 35

Vos Old
Testament
Lessons 18-23

Hurlbut Part 1
Lessons 13

our God
אֱלֹהֵינוּ
eloheynu

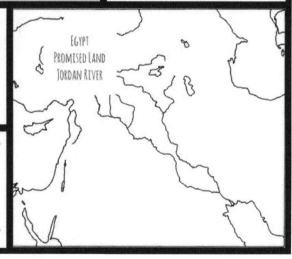

Egypt
Promised Land
Jordan River

BIBLE FACTS

THE STATUE IN DANIEL, V. 1

To the tune of "Joyful, Joyful"

Nebuchadnezzar has a bad dream,

Daniel tells him what it means,

A statue made of five parts tells the

Empires to come on the scene:

Head of gold is Babylon,

Persia: silver arms and chest.

Greece: the belly and thighs made of bronze,

Roman Empire: iron legs.

TIMELINE

Joseph in Egypt

Moses' Life

Burning bush
and plagues in
Egypt

_A_	_M_	_D_	_E_
2000	1500	1000	500

hymn

ROCK OF AGES
verse 1

Rock of Ages, cleft for me,
let me hide myself in Thee;
let the water and the blood,
from Thy wounded side
which flowed,
be of sin the double cure;
save from wrath
and make me pure.

I PRACTICED:

☆ ☆ ☆ ☆ ☆ ☆

M	T	W	T	F	S
O	U	E	H	R	A
N	E	D	U	I	T

CYCLE 11
BURNING BUSH
PLAGUES IN EGYPT
WEEK 5

PROVERBS 3:5

Trust in the Lord
with all your heart

and lean not on
your own
understanding;

related stories

Exodus 3-12

Vos Old
Testament
Lessons 33-34

Hurlbut Part 1
Lessons 21-23

Yahweh

יהוה

Yahweh

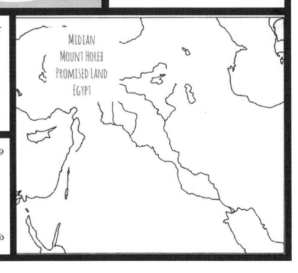

MIDIAN
MOUNT HOREB
PROMISED LAND
EGYPT

BIBLE FACTS
The Statue in Daniel, v. 2
To the tune of "Joyful, Joyful"

Feet and toes of clay and iron:

A kingdom yet-to-transpire,

A rock that's cut out from a mountain,

Will consume all these empires.

God will set up His own Kingdom,

It shall never be destroyed.

Worship Him, our source of freedom,

He is all our hope and joy.

TIMELINE

Exodus and 10 Commandments

Desert, Ark, Feasts, Tabernacle

Joshua's Conquest

_A_	_M_	_D___	_E__
2000	1500	1000	500

hymn

ROCK OF AGES
verse 2

Not the labors of my hands

can fulfill Thy law's demands;

could my zeal no respite know,

could my tears forever flow,

all for sin could not atone;

Thou must save, and Thou alone.

I PRACTICED:

☆ ☆ ☆ ☆ ☆ ☆

M	T	W	T	F	S
O	U	E	H	R	A
N	E	D	U	I	T

CYCLE 11
JOSHUA'S CONQUEST
WEEK 6

PROVERBS 3:6

in all your ways
submit to Him,
and He will
make your paths
straight.

related stories

Joshua 1-24

Vos Old Testament Lessons 53-56

Hurlbut Part 2 Lessons 1-5

(is) one

אֶחָד

echad

REUBEN
SIMEON
JUDAH
ISSACHAR
ZEBULUN
EPHRAIM
MANNASEH
BENJAMIN
NAPHTALI
DAN
GAD
ASHER

BIBLE FACTS
The Statue in Daniel, v. 1-2
To the tune of "Joyful, Joyful"

Nebuchadnezzar has a bad dream,
Daniel tells him what it means,
A statue made of five parts tells the
Empires to come on the scene:
Head of gold is Babylon,
Persia: silver arms and chest.
Greece: the belly and thighs made of bronze,
Roman Empire: iron legs.

Feet and toes of clay and iron:
A kingdom yet-to-transpire,
A rock that's cut out from a mountain,
Will consume all these empires.
God will set up His own Kingdom,
It shall never be destroyed.
Worship Him, our source of freedom,
He is all our hope and joy.

TIMELINE

Judges rule

Ruth and Boaz

King Saul's reign

_A_____	M_____	D_____	E_
2000	1500	1000	500

hymn

ROCK OF AGES
verse 3

Nothing in my hand I bring,

simply to the cross I cling;

naked, come to Thee for dress;

helpless, look to Thee for grace;

foul, I to the fountain fly;

wash me, Savior, or I die.

I PRACTICED:

☆ ☆ ☆ ☆ ☆ ☆

M	T	W	T	F	S
O	U	E	H	R	A
N	E	D	U	I	T

CYCLE 11
KING SAUL'S REIGN
WEEK 7

PROVERBS 3:7

Do not be wise
in your own eyes;

fear the Lord
and shun evil.

related stories
1 Samuel 8-31

Vos Old
Testament
Lessons 65-71

Hurlbut Part 2
Lesson 18
Part 3 Lessons 1-9

Hear, O Israel,
Yahweh, our
Yahweh (is) one.
שְׁמַע יִשְׂרָאֵל יְהוָה
אֱלֹהֵינוּ יְהוָה אֶחָד
Shema Yisrael
Yahweh eloheynu
Yahweh echad

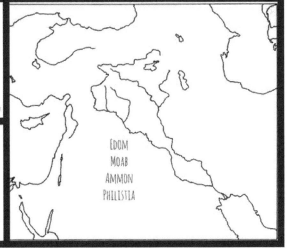

EDOM
MOAB
AMMON
PHILISTIA

BIBLE FACTS

The Statue in Daniel, v. 1-2

To the tune of "Joyful, Joyful"

Nebuchadnezzar has a bad dream,
Daniel tells him what it means,
A statue made of five parts tells the
Empires to come on the scene:
Head of gold is Babylon,
Persia: silver arms and chest.
Greece: the belly and thighs made of bronze,
Roman Empire: iron legs.

Feet and toes of clay and iron:
A kingdom yet-to-transpire,
A rock that's cut out from a mountain,
Will consume all these empires.
God will set up His own Kingdom,
It shall never be destroyed.
Worship Him, our source of freedom,
He is all our hope and joy.

TIMELINE

David's Kingdom

Psalms, Covenant

Solomon's Temple,
Kingdom divides

A	M	D	E
2000	1500	1000	500

hymn

ROCK OF AGES
verse 4

While I draw this fleeting breath,

when mine eyes

shall close in death,

when I soar to worlds unknown,

see Thee on

Thy judgment throne,

Rock of Ages, cleft for me,

let me hide myself in Thee.

I PRACTICED:

☆ ☆ ☆ ☆ ☆ ☆

M	T	W	T	F	S
O	U	E	H	R	A
N	E	D	U	I	T

CYCLE 11
SOLOMON'S TEMPLE
KINGDOM DIVIDES
WEEK 8

PROVERBS 3:8

This will bring
health to your body

and nourishment
to your bones.

related stories

1 Kings 2-13

Vos Old
Testament
Lessons 76-79

Hurlbut Part 3
Lessons 17-20,
Part 4 Lesson 1

Blessed

בָּרוּךְ

Barukh

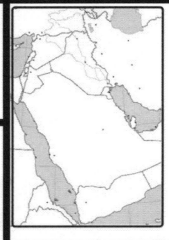

Jerusalem
Lebanon
Sheba

BIBLE FACTS
Review The Tabernacle and the Names of God
To the tunes of "If You're Happy" and "Away in a Manger"

Inside the Tabernacle:	Elohim: Creator, El Roi: God who Sees,
	El Shaddai means God Almighty,
Were Bronze Altar	Jehovah Nissi: The Lord our Banner,
	Jehovah Rohi: The Lord our Shepherd.
and Lampstand of gold	
	Jehovah Jirah: The Lord Will Provide,
Mercy Seat,	El El-yon means God Most High,
	El Olam means God Everlasting,
Bronze Laver,	Jehovah Rapha: The Lord who Heals.
And the	Jehovah Shalom: The Lord is our Peace,
	Adonai means Lord Almighty,
Showbread table	Your Sanctifier: Jehovah Maccaddeshem, Jehovah
	Tsidkenu: Our righteousness.
Ark of Covenant	
	Jehovah Sabbaoth: Lord of Hosts everywhere,
Incense Altar of gold.	Jehovah Shammah: The Lord who is there,
	Abba means Papa, Mighty God: El Gibhor,
	Speak reverently, these are the Names of the Lord.

TIMELINE

Ahab and Elijah on the north side

Hezekiah and Isaiah in the South

Israel falls to Assyria's clout

A	M	D	E
2000	1500	1000	500

hymn

BATTLE HYMN OF THE REPUBLIC
verse 1

Mine eyes have seen the glory of the
coming of the Lord;
He is trampling out the vintage
where the grapes of wrath are stored;
He has loosed the fateful lightning of
His terrible swift sword,
His truth is marching on.
Refrain:
Glory, glory hallelujah!
Glory, glory hallelujah!
Glory, glory hallelujah!
His truth is marching on.

I PRACTICED:

☆ ☆ ☆ ☆ ☆ ☆

M	T	W	T	F	S
O	U	E	H	R	A
N	E	D	U	I	T

CYCLE 11
ISRAEL FALLS TO ASSYRIA
WEEK 9

PROVERBS 3:9

Honor the Lord
with your wealth,

with the firstfruits
of all your crops;

related stories

2 Kings 15

Vos Old
Testament
Lesson 94

Hurlbut Part 4
Lessons 17-18

(the) name
(of)
שֵׁם
shem

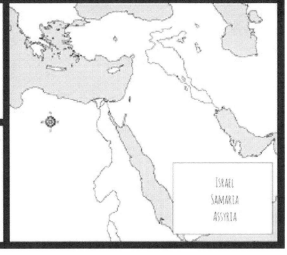

ISRAEL
SAMARIA
ASSYRIA

BIBLE FACTS
Review the Offerings and Covenants
To the tunes of "Michael Finnegan" and "The Old Grey Mare"

Peace or
fellowship
offerings,
Meal/grain
offerings,
Burnt
offerings,
Trespass or
guilt offerings,
Sin offerings.

God made many promises called covenants,
The first, the Adamic, says a Savior will be sent,
Noahic says there won't again be sent
A flood to destroy the earth.

Abrahamic Covenant pledged at God's command:
A great name, a nation, and a promised land,
Descendants just as numerous as sand,
A blessing to all the earth.

Mosaic says obey the law and you'll be fine.
Davidic: an eternal king from David's line,
New Covenant: I will make this people mine
God's promise to all the earth!

TIMELINE

Jeremiah and Ezekiel
warn Judah

Judah falls to Babylon,
Temple ruined

Daniel in the Exile

A	M	D	E
2000	1500	1000	500

hymn

BATTLE HYMN OF THE REPUBLIC
verse 2

I have seen Him in the watch-fires
of a hundred circling camps,
They have builded Him an altar in
the evening dews and damps;
I can read His righteous sentence
by the dim and flaring lamps:
His day is marching on.
[Refrain]

I PRACTICED:
☆ ☆ ☆ ☆ ☆ ☆
M	T	W	T	F	S
O	U	E	H	R	A
N	E	D	U	I	T

CYCLE 11
DANIEL IN THE EXILE
WEEK 10

PROVERBS 3:10

then your barns
will be filled
to overflowing,

and your vats
will brim over
with new wine.

related stories
Daniel 1-12
Vos Old
Testament
Lessons 100-104
Hurlbut Part 5
Lessons 8-12

glorious
kingdom
כְּבוֹד מַלְכוּת
kevod
malkuto

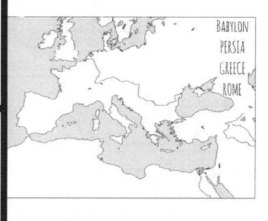

BABYLON
PERSIA
GREECE
ROME

BIBLE FACTS

Review the Judges and the Sons of Israel

To the tunes of "Jesus Loves Me" and "Jacob's Ladder"

Othniel, Ehud, Shamgar,

Deborah, Gideon, Abimelech,

Tola, Jair,

Jephthah, Ibzan, Elon, Abdon,

Samson, Eli, Samuel

Judges of Israel,

Judges of Israel,

Judges of Israel,

Because God was their King.

- Reuben
- Simeon
- Levi
- Judah
- Issachar
- Zebulon
- Joseph
- Benjamin
- Dan
- Naphtali
- Gad
- and Asher,
  Sons of Israel

TIMELINE

Cyrus' decree
Exiles return

Temple rebuilding

Esther saves the
Jews

A	M	D	E
2000	1500	1000	500

hymn

BATTLE HYMN OF THE
REPUBLIC
verse 3

He has sounded forth the trumpet
that shall never call retreat
He is sifting out the hearts of men
before His judgment seat;
O be swift, my soul, to answer Him;
O be jubilant my feet!
Our God is marching on.
[Refrain]

I PRACTICED:

☆ ☆ ☆ ☆ ☆ ☆

M	T	W	T	F	S
O	U	E	H	R	A
N	E	D	U	I	T

CYCLE 11

ESTHER SAVES THE JEWS

WEEK 11

PROVERBS 3:11

My son,
do not despise
the Lord's discipline,

and do not resent
His rebuke,

related stories

Esther 1-10

Vos Old
Testament
Lessons 107-108

Hurlbut Part 5
Lesson 15

forever and
ever

לְעוֹלָם וָעֶד

l'olam va-ed

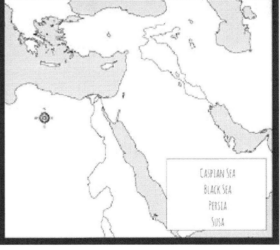

Caspian Sea
Black Sea
Persia
Susa

BIBLE FACTS

Review

Feasts of the Lord

Passover: Saved by the blood of the lamb,

Unleavened Bread: Dead to sin, I am

Firstfruits: Celebrates life from the ground

Pentecost: Making laws and vows

Rosh Hashanah: New Year trumpets play

Yom Kippur: Atonement day

Tabernacles: Joy and peace

These are God's Appointed Feasts

Books of the Old Testament

Genesis, Exodus, Leviticus, Numbers, Deuteronomy, Joshua, Judges, Ruth, First and Second Samuel, First Kings, Second Kings, First and Second Chronicles, Ezra, Nehemiah, Esther, Job, Psalms, Proverbs, Ecclesiastes, Song of Solomon, Isaiah, Jeremiah, Lamentations, Ezekiel, Daniel, Hosea, Joel, Amos, Obadiah, Jonah, Micah, Nahum, Habakkuk, Zephaniah, Haggai, Zechariah, and the last one, Malachi

TIMELINE

Nehemiah builds the wall

Malachi foretells John the Baptist's call

Maccabean period ends here, no word from God for 400 years

A	M	D	E
2000	1500	1000	500

hymn

BATTLE HYMN OF THE REPUBLIC
verse 4

In the beauty of the lilies
Christ was born across the sea,
with a glory in His bosom that
transfigures you and me;
as He died to make men holy,
let us live to make men free,
while God is marching on.
[Refrain]

I PRACTICED:

☆ ☆ ☆ ☆ ☆ ☆

M	T	W	T	F	S
O	U	E	H	R	A
N	E	D	U	I	T

CYCLE 11
MACCABEAN PERIOD
WEEK 12

PROVERBS 3:12

because the Lord disciplines those He loves,

as a father the son he delights in.

related stories

Hurlbut Part 5
Lesson 16

Blessed be the name of His glorious kingdom forever and ever.
בָּרוּךְ שֵׁם כְּבוֹד מַלְכוּתוֹ לְעוֹלָם וָעֶד
Barukh shem kevod malkuto l'olam va-ed.

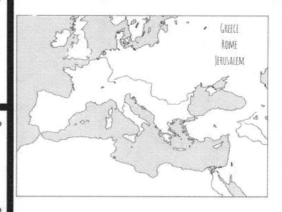

GREECE
ROME
JERUSALEM

BIBLE FACTS

The Lord's Prayer

MUSIC USED BY PERMISSION FROM ALBERT HAY MALOTTE

Our Father, which art in heaven, hallowed be Thy name;
Thy kingdom come; Thy will be done,
In earth as it is in heaven.

Give us this day our daily bread.
And forgive us our debts, as we forgive our debtors
And lead us not into temptation; but deliver us from evil.

For Thine is the kingdom, and the power, and the glory,
For ever and ever. Amen.

TIMELINE

John the Baptist

Messiah is born

Shepherds and
Magi visit the Lord

J	R	P	T	R
-5	33	46-58	70	96

hymn

ALAS, AND DID MY SAVIOR BLEED?
verse 1

Alas! and did my Savior bleed,

and did my Sovereign die!

Would He devote

that sacred head

for sinners such as I?

I PRACTICED:

☆ ☆ ☆ ☆ ☆ ☆

M	T	W	T	F	S
O	U	E	H	R	A
N	E	D	U	I	T

CYCLE 12
SHEPHERDS AND MAGI
WEEK 1

1 CORINTHIANS 15:50

I declare to you, brothers
and sisters, that flesh and
blood cannot inherit the
kingdom of God, nor does
the perishable inherit the
imperishable.

related stories

Matthew 2
Luke 2

Vos New
Testament
Lesson 4

Hurlbut Part 6
Lessons 2-3

(the) God

ὁ θεός

(o) theós

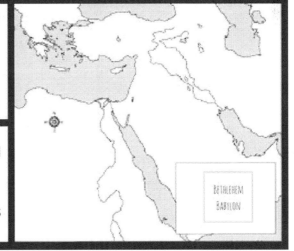

BETHLEHEM
BABYLON

BIBLE FACTS

The Lord's Prayer

Music used by permission from Albert Hay Malotte

Our Father, which art in heaven, hallowed be Thy name;

Thy kingdom come; Thy will be done,

In earth as it is in heaven.

Give us this day our daily bread.

And forgive us our debts, as we forgive our debtors

And lead us not into temptation; but deliver us from evil.

For Thine is the kingdom, and the power, and the glory,

For ever and ever. Amen.

TIMELINE

Flight into Egypt
Herod's Slaughter

Boy Jesus at the Temple

Baptism at the Jordan

J	R	P	T	R
-5	33	46-58	70	96

hymn

ALAS, AND DID
MY SAVIOR BLEED
verse 2

Was it for crimes that I have done,

He groaned upon the tree?

Amazing pity! Grace unknown!

And love beyond degree!

I PRACTICED:

☆ ☆ ☆ ☆ ☆ ☆

M	T	W	T	F	S
O	U	E	H	R	A
N	E	D	U	I	T

CYCLE 12

BAPTISM AT JORDAN

WEEK 2

1 CORINTHIANS 15:51

Listen, I tell you a mystery:

We will not all sleep, but we will all be changed—

related stories

Matthew 3

Vos New Testament Lesson 7

Hurlbut Part 6 Lesson 6

is

είναι

eínai

(EE-ne)

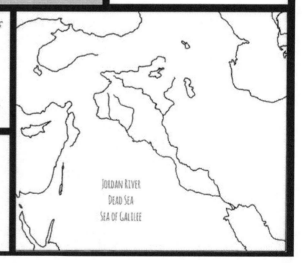

Jordan River
Dead Sea
Sea of Galilee

BIBLE FACTS

The Lord's Prayer

Music used by permission from Albert Hay Malotte

Our Father, which art in heaven, hallowed be Thy name;

Thy kingdom come; Thy will be done,

In earth as it is in heaven.

Give us this day our daily bread.

And forgive us our debts, as we forgive our debtors

And lead us not into temptation; but deliver us from evil.

For Thine is the kingdom, and the power, and the glory,

For ever and ever. Amen.

TIMELINE

Temptation in the desert

Disciples' Call

Cana Wedding
Jubilee Inaugural

J	R	P	T	R
-5	33	46-58	70	96

hymn

ALAS, AND DID MY SAVIOR BLEED
verse 3

Well might the sun in darkness hide,

and shut its glories in,

when God, the mighty Maker, died

for His own creatures" sin.

I PRACTICED:

☆ ☆ ☆ ☆ ☆ ☆

M	T	W	T	F	S
O	U	E	H	R	A
N	E	D	U	I	T

CYCLE 12
CANA WEDDING
JUBILEE INAUGURAL
WEEK 3

1 CORINTHIANS 15:52

in a flash, in the twinkling of an eye, at the last trumpet.

For the trumpet will sound, the dead will be raised imperishable, and we will be changed.

related stories

Luke 4
John 2

Vos New Testament Lesson 10

Hurlbut Part 6
Lessons 7, 9

love

αγάπη

agápi

CANA
CAPERNAUM
NAZARETH

BIBLE FACTS

The Lord's Prayer

Music used by permission from Albert Hay Malotte

Our Father, which art in heaven, hallowed be Thy name;

Thy kingdom come; Thy will be done,

In earth as it is in heaven.

Give us this day our daily bread.

And forgive us our debts, as we forgive our debtors

And lead us not into temptation; but deliver us from evil.

For Thine is the kingdom, and the power, and the glory,

For ever and ever. Amen.

TIMELINE

Jesus clears the Temple, Ministry begins

Meets Nicodemus and the Samaritan

Sermon on the Mount

J	R	P	T	R
-5	33	46-58	70	96

hymn

ALAS, AND DID
MY SAVIOR BLEED
verse 4

Thus might I hide my blushing face

while His dear cross appears;

dissolve my heart in thankfulness,

and melt mine eyes to tears.

I PRACTICED:

☆ ☆ ☆ ☆ ☆ ☆

M	T	W	T	F	S
O	U	E	H	R	A
N	E	D	U	I	T

CYCLE 12
Sermon on the Mount
WEEK 4

1 CORINTHIANS 15:53

For the perishable must clothe itself with the imperishable,

and the mortal with immortality.

related stories

Matthew 5-7

Vos New Testament Lesson 20

Hurlbut Part 6 Lesson 13

God is love.

Ο Θεός είναι αγάπη.

O Theós eínai agápi.

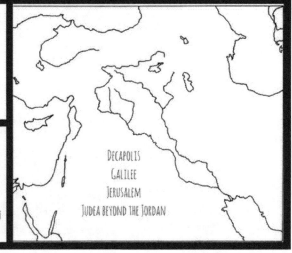

Decapolis
Galilee
Jerusalem
Judea beyond the Jordan

BIBLE FACTS

The Armor of God

To the tune of "Itsy Bitsy Spider"

Belt of truth, buckled around your waist,

Breastplate of righteousness in place,

Feet fitted with the Gospel of Peace,

With the shield of faith, the devil's fiery darts will cease.

With the helmet of salvation your head must be shod,

The sword of the Spirit, which is the Word of God,

Here's your protection from the devil's tricks,

The Armor of God, found in Ephesians six.

CYCLE 12

MIRACLES

WEEK 5

TIMELINE

Jesus feeds 5000,

Transfiguration,

Miracles abounding

J	R	P	T	R
-5	33	46-58	70	96

hymn

ALAS, AND DID
MY SAVIOR BLEED
verse 5

But drops of tears can

ne'er repay

the debt of love I owe.

Here, Lord, I give

myself away:

'tis all that I can do.

1 CORINTHIANS 15:54

When the perishable has been clothed with the imperishable, and the mortal with immortality, then the saying that is written will come true: "Death has been swallowed up in victory."

related stories
Mark 1

Vos New Testament Lessons 14-7, 19, 21, 23-4, 27-9, 38

Hurlbut Part 6 Lesson 14, 16-7, 24, 26

In (the) beginning

Ἐν ἀρχῇ

En ar-KAY

Jerusalem
Nazareth
Capernaum
Syria

BIBLE FACTS

The Armor of God

To the tune of "Itsy Bitsy Spider"

Belt of truth, buckled around your waist,

Breastplate of righteousness in place,

Feet fitted with the Gospel of Peace,

With the shield of faith, the devil's fiery darts will cease.

With the helmet of salvation your head must be shod,

The sword of the Spirit, which is the Word of God,

Here's your protection from the devil's tricks,

The Armor of God, found in Ephesians six.

I PRACTICED:

☆ ☆ ☆ ☆ ☆ ☆

M	T	W	T	F	S
O	U	E	H	R	A
N	E	D	U	I	T

CYCLE 12
OLIVET DISCOURSE
WEEK 6

TIMELINE

Parables

Triumphal Entry

Olivet Discourse on

things to be

J	R	P	T	R
-5	33	46-58	70	96

hymn

CHRIST THE LORD IS RISEN TODAY
verse 1

Christ the Lord is risen today,

Alleluia!

Sons of men and angels say,

Alleluia!

Raise your joys and triumphs high,

Alleluia!

Sing, ye heavens, and earth reply,

Alleluia!

1 CORINTHIANS 15:55

"Where, O death, is your victory?

Where, O death, is your sting?"

related stories

Matthew 24-25

Vos New Testament Lesson 43

Hurlbut Part 6 Lesson 32

was the Word

ἦν ὁ λόγος

ayn ha LOH-gohs

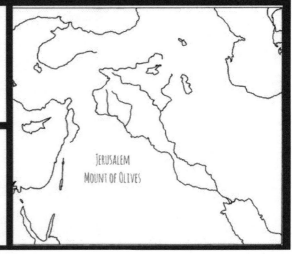

Jerusalem
Mount of Olives

BIBLE FACTS
The Armor of God
To the tune of "Itsy Bitsy Spider"

Belt of truth, buckled around your waist,

Breastplate of righteousness in place,

Feet fitted with the Gospel of Peace,

With the shield of faith, the devil's fiery darts will cease.

With the helmet of salvation your head must be shod,

The sword of the Spirit, which is the Word of God,

Here's your protection from the devil's tricks,

The Armor of God, found in Ephesians six.

TIMELINE

Last Passover

Crucifixion

Resurrection

J	R	P	T	R
-5	33	46-58	70	96

hymn

CHRIST THE LORD IS RISEN TODAY
verse 2

Love's redeeming work is done,
Alleluia!
Fought the fight, the battle won,
Alleluia!
Death in vain forbids Him rise,
Alleluia!
Christ has opened paradise,
Alleluia!

I PRACTICED:
☆ ☆ ☆ ☆ ☆ ☆

M	T	W	T	F	S
O	U	E	H	R	A
N	E	D	U	I	T

CYCLE 12
RESURRECTION
WEEK 7

1 CORINTHIANS 15:56

The sting of death is sin,

and the power of sin is the law.

related stories
Luke 24 John 20

Vos New Testament Lessons 52-54

Hurlbut Part 6 Lesson 37

and the Word

καὶ ὁ λόγος

kī ha LOH-gohs

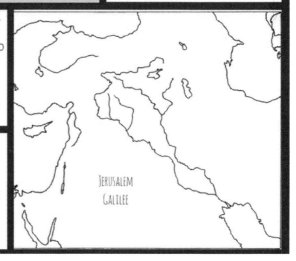

Jerusalem
Galilee

BIBLE FACTS
The Armor of God
To the tune of "Itsy Bitsy Spider"

Belt of truth, buckled around your waist,

Breastplate of righteousness in place,

Feet fitted with the Gospel of Peace,

With the shield of faith, the devil's fiery darts will cease.

With the helmet of salvation your head must be shod,

The sword of the Spirit, which is the Word of God,

Here's your protection from the devil's tricks,

The Armor of God, found in Ephesians six.

TIMELINE
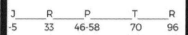

Ascension

Pentecost, Holy Spirit received

Peter preaches, 3,000 believe

J	R	P	T	R
-5	33	46-58	70	96

hymn

CHRIST THE LORD
IS RISEN TODAY
verse 3

Lives again our glorious King,

Alleluia!

Where, O death, is now thy sting?

Alleluia!

Once He died our souls to save,

Alleluia!

Where thy victory, O grave?

Alleluia!

I PRACTICED:

☆ ☆ ☆ ☆ ☆ ☆

M	T	W	T	F	S
O	U	E	H	R	A
N	E	D	U	I	T

CYCLE 12
PETER PREACHES
3,000 BELIEVE
WEEK 8

1 CORINTHIANS 15:57

But thanks be to God!

He gives us the victory through our Lord Jesus Christ.!

related stories
Acts 2

Vos New Testament Lessons 57-60, 62, 67, 70

Hurlbut Part 7 Lessons 2, 3, 5, 7, 8

was with the God

ἦν πρὸς τὸν θεόν

ayn pros ton theos

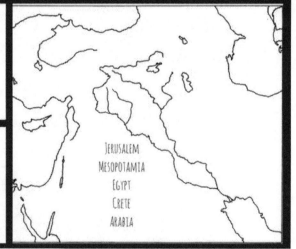

Jerusalem
Mesopotamia
Egypt
Crete
Arabia

BIBLE FACTS
REVIEW!

ATTRIBUTES OF GOD

God's eternal, infinite,
Self-existent, self-sufficient,
God is omnipresent,
And omniscient.

God is immutable
Sovereign, wise, holy, good,
Righteous, just, faithful and true,
God is triune.

God is gracious, merciful,
He is spirit and life too,
God is omnipotent,
God is love, it's true!

JESUS' MIRACLES

The Lord turned water
into wine,
Healed the sick,
deaf, dumb and blind,
Cast out demons,
calmed the sea,
Raised the dead,
killed a tree.
Healed the lame,
Cured leprosy,
Restored a withered limb
and a severed ear,
Two enormous crowds
He fed,
Walked on water,
Rose from the dead.

TIMELINE

Stephen martyred

Conversion of Saul

Paul's first journey

J	R	P	T	R
-5	33	46-58	70	96

hymn

CHRIST THE LORD
IS RISEN TODAY
verse 4

Soar we now where Christ has led,
Alleluia!
Following our exalted Head,
Alleluia!
Made like Him, like Him we rise,
Alleluia!
Ours the cross, the grave, the skies,
Alleluia!

I PRACTICED:

☆ ☆ ☆ ☆ ☆

M	T	W	T	F	S
O	U	E	H	R	A
N	E	D	U	I	T

CYCLE 12
PAUL'S FIRST JOURNEY
WEEK 9

1 CORINTHIANS 15:58

Therefore, my dear
brothers and sisters,
stand firm. Let nothing
move you. Always give
yourselves fully to the
work of the Lord,
because you know that
your labor in the Lord is
not in vain.

related stories

Acts 13-14

Vos New
Testament
Lessons 71-72

Hurlbut Part 7
Lesson 9

and God

καὶ θεὸς

kī theos

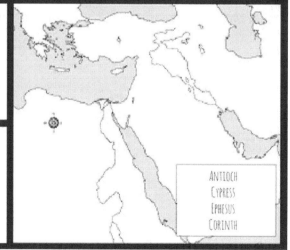

ANTIOCH
CYPRESS
EPHESUS
CORINTH

BIBLE FACTS
REVIEW!

THE LORD'S PRAYER

Our Father, which art in heaven,
hallowed be Thy name;
Thy kingdom come;
Thy will be done,
In earth as it is in heaven.

Give us this day our daily bread.
And forgive us our debts,
as we forgive our debtors
And lead us not into temptation;
but deliver us from evil.

For Thine is the kingdom,
and the power,
and the glory,
For ever and ever.
Amen.

THE CHURCHES IN REVELATION

Revelation

churches

are:

Ephesus,

Smyrna,

Pergamon,

Thyatira,

Sardis,

Philadelphia,

Laodicea,

seven in all!

TIMELINE

Jerusalem Council

Paul's Second Journey

Thessalonians, Galatians, Romans, Corinthians

J	R	P	T	R
-5	33	46-58	70	96

---

hymn

FAITH OF OUR FATHERS
verse 1

Faith of our fathers! living still

in spite of dungeon, fire, and sword;

oh, how our hearts

beat high with joy

whene'er we hear

that glorious word!

Faith of our fathers, holy faith!

We will be true to thee till death!

I PRACTICED:

☆ ☆ ☆ ☆ ☆ ☆

M	T	W	T	F	S
O	U	E	H	R	A
N	E	D	U	I	T

CYCLE 12
THESSALONIANS, GALATIANS, ROMANS, CORINTHIANS
WEEK 10

JOHN 14:1

Do not let your hearts be troubled.

You believe in God; believe also in Me.

---

related stories

Thessalonians, Galatians, Romans, Corinthians

Hurlbut Part 7 Lesson 13

---

was the Word

ἦν ὁ λόγος

nee logos

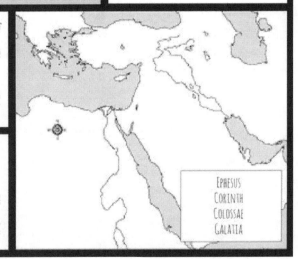

EPHESUS
CORINTH
COLOSSAE
GALATIA

BIBLE FACTS
REVIEW!
Catechism Q. 1-5

Q. 1 What is the chief end of man?

A. 1 Man's chief end is to glorify God, and to enjoy Him forever.

Q. 2 What rule has God given to direct us how we may glorify and enjoy Him?

A. 2 The word of God, namely the Scriptures of the Old and New Testaments, is the only rule to direct us how we may glorify and enjoy Him.

Q. 3 Are the Scriptures trustworthy in all that they affirm?

A. 3 The Scriptures of both the Old and New Testaments, being Godbreathed, are infallible and inerrant in all their parts and are, therefore, trustworthy in all that they affirm concerning history, science, doctrine, ethics, religious practice, or any other topic.

Q. 4 What do the Scriptures principally teach?

A. 4 The Scriptures principally teach what man is to believe concerning God, and what duty God requires of man.

Q. 5 What is God?

A. 5 God is a Spirit, infinite, eternal, and unchangeable, in His being, wisdom, power, holiness, justice, goodness, and truth.

TIMELINE

Paul sent to prison

Paul stands trial

Paul shipwrecked on an isle

J	R	P	T	R
-5	33	46-58	70	96

hymn

FAITH OF OUR FATHERS
verse 2

I PRACTICED:

☆ ☆ ☆ ☆ ☆ ☆

M	T	W	T	F	S
O	U	E	H	R	A
N	E	D	U	I	T

CYCLE 12

PAUL SHIPWRECKED

WEEK 11

JOHN 14:2

My Father's house has many rooms; if that were not so, would I have told you that I am going there to prepare a place for you?

related stories

Acts 27-28

Vos New Testament Lessons 88-91

Hurlbut Part 7 Lesson 18

God is love.

Ο Θεός είναι αγάπη.

O Theós eínai agápi.

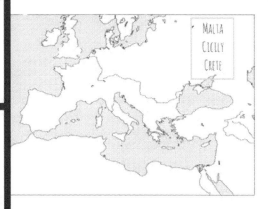

MALTA
CICILY
CRETE

BIBLE FACTS
REVIEW!
Catechism Q. 6, 7, 9-11

Q. 6 Are there more Gods than one?
A. 6 There is but one only, the living and true God.

Q. 7 How many persons are there in the Godhead?
A. 7 There are three persons in the Godhead: the Father, the Son, and the Holy Spirit; and these three are one God, the same in substance, equal in power and glory.

Q. 9 How does God execute His decrees?
A. 9 God executes His decrees in the works of creation and providence.

Q. 10 What is the work of creation?
A. 10 The work of creation is God's making all things of nothing, by the word of His power, in the space of six days, and all very good.

Q. 11 How did God create man?
A. 11 God created man, male and female, after His own image, in knowledge, righteousness, and holiness, with dominion over the creatures.

TIMELINE

Paul writes more letters from prison

Titus sacks the Temple

Revelation vision

J	R	P	T	R
-5	33	46-58	70	96

hymn

FAITH OF OUR FATHERS
verse 3

Faith of our fathers! we will love

both friend and foe in all our strife;

and preach thee, too,

as love knows how,

by kindly words and virtuous life:

faith of our fathers, holy faith!

We will be true to thee till death!

I PRACTICED:

☆ ☆ ☆ ☆ ☆ ☆

M	T	W	T	F	S
O	U	E	H	R	A
N	E	D	U	I	T

CYCLE 12
REVELATION VISION
WEEK 12

JOHN 14:3

And if I go
and prepare a place
for you,
I will come back
and take you
to be with Me
that you also may be
where I am.

related stories

Revelation 1-22

Vos
New Testament
Lesson 92

Hurlbut Part 7
Lessons 20-21

In the beginning was
the Word,
and the Word was
with God
and God was
the Word.

Ἐν ἀρχῇ ἦν
ὁ λόγος,
καὶ ὁ λόγος ἦν
πρὸς τὸν θεόν,
καὶ θεὸς ἦν
ὁ λόγος

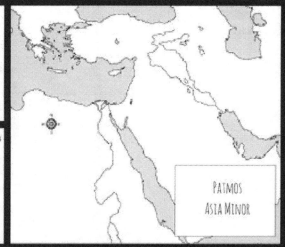

Patmos
Asia Minor

Old Testament Timeline

Creation, Fall, Cain and Abel,
Flood, Job, Tower of Babel,
Abraham, Ishmael,
Sodom and Gomorrah, Isaac as Well.

Jacob and Esau, Israel's Tribes,
Joseph in Egypt, Moses' Life,
Burning Bush and Plagues in Egypt,
Exodus and Ten Commandments.

Desert, Ark, Feasts, Tabernacle,
Joshua's Conquest, Judges Rule,
Ruth and Boaz, King Saul's Reign,
David's Kingdom, Psalms, Covenant.

Solomon's Temple, Kingdom Divides,
Ahab and Elijah on the North Side,
Hezekiah and Isaiah in the South,
Israel Falls to Assyria's Clout.

Jeremiah and Ezekiel Warn Judah,
Judah Falls To Babylon,
Temple Ruined
Daniel in the Exile, Cyrus' Decree,
Exiles Return, Temple Rebuilding.

Esther Saves the Jews,
Nehemiah Builds the Wall,
Malachi Foretells John the Baptist's Call,
Maccabean Period Ends Here,
No Word from God for 400 Years.

Statue in Daniel

Nebuchadnezzar has a bad dream,
Daniel tells him what it means,
A statue made of five parts tells the
Empires to come on the scene:
Head of gold is Babylon,
Persia: silver arms and chest,
Greece: the belly and thighs made
    of bronze,
Roman Empire: iron legs.

Feet and toes of clay and iron:
A kingdom yet -to -transpire,
A rock that's cut out from
    a mountain,
Will consume all these empires.
God will set up His own Kingdom,
It shall never be destroyed.
Worship Him, our source
    of freedom,
He is all our hope and joy.

Hymns

Joyful, Joyful, We Adore Thee
Rock of Ages
Battle Hymn of the Republic

Hebrew Calendar

Nisan, Iyar,

Sivan, Tammuz,

Av, Elul,

Tishri, Heshvan,

Kislev, Teveth,

Shevat, Adar,

and Adar Bet

Hebrew Alphabet

Handy Hebrew Writing Guide - Block Printing			
ד	ג	ב	א
Dalet	Gimmel	Bet	Aleph
ח	ז	ו	ה
Chet	Zayin	Vav	Hey
ך	כ	י	ט
Final Kaf	Kaf	Yod	Tet
נ	מ	מ	ל
Nun	Final Mem	Mem	Lamed
פ	ע	ס	ן
Pey	Ayin	Samech	Final Nun
ק	צ	צ	ף
Qof	Final Tzade	Tzade	Final Pey
ת	ש	ר	
Tav	Shin	Resh	

Proverbs 3:1-12

My son, do not forget my teaching,
    but keep my commands in your heart,

for they will prolong your life many years
    and bring you peace and prosperity.

Let love and faithfulness never leave you;
bind them around your neck, write them
    on the tablet of your heart.

Then you will win favor and a good name
    in the sight of God and man.

Trust in the Lord with all your heart
    and lean not on your own understanding;

In all your ways submit to Him,
    and He will make your paths straight.

Do not be wise in your own eyes;
    fear the Lord and shun evil.

This will bring health to your body
    and nourishment to your bones.

Honor the Lord with your wealth,
    with the firstfruits of all your crops;

Then your barns will be filled to
overflowing, and your vats will brim over
with new wine.

My son, do not despise the Lord's
discipline, and do not resent His rebuke,

because the Lord disciplines those He
loves, as a father the son he delights in.

The Shema

Hear, O Israel, Yahweh our God,
Yahweh is one.
Blessed be the name of His
glorious kingdom forever and
ever.

שְׁמַע יִשְׂרָאֵל יהוה אֱלֹהֵינוּ יהוה אֶחָד
בָּרוּךְ שֵׁם כְּבוֹד מַלְכוּתוֹ לְעוֹלָם וָעֶד

Shema, Yisrael, Yahweh
eloheynu, Yahweh echad.

Barukh shem kevod malkuto
l'olam va-ed.

New Testament Timeline

John the Baptist, Messiah Is Born,
Shepherds and Magi Visit the Lord,
Flight into Egypt, Herod's Slaughter,
Boy Jesus at the Temple,
Baptism at the Jordan.

Temptation in the Desert,
Disciples' Call, Cana Wedding,
Jubilee Inaugural
Jesus Clears the Temple,
Ministry Begins,
Meets Nicodemus and the Samaritan.

Sermon on the Mount,
Jesus Feeds 5000,
Transfiguration, Miracles Abounding,
Parables, Triumphal Entry,
Olivet Discourse on Things to Be.

Last Passover, Crucifixion,
Resurrection, Ascension,
Pentecost, Holy Spirit Received,
Peter Preaches, 3000 Believe.

Stephen Martyred, Conversion of Saul,
Paul's First Journey, Jerusalem Council,
Paul's Second Journey, Thessalonians,
Romans, Galatians, Corinthians.

Paul Sent to Prison, Paul Stands Trial,
Paul Shipwrecked on an Isle,
Paul Writes More Letters from Prison,
Titus Sacks the Temple,
Revelation Vision.

The Lord's Prayer

Our Father, which art in heaven,
hallowed be thy name;
thy kingdom come;
thy will be done,
in earth as it is in heaven.
Give us this day our daily bread.
And forgive us our debts,
as we forgive our debtors.
And lead us not into temptation;
but deliver us from evil.
For thine is the kingdom,
the power, and the glory,
for ever and ever.
Amen.

Armor of God

Belt of truth, buckled around your waist,
Breastplate of righteousness in place.
Feet fitted with the Gospel of Peace.
With the shield of faith,
the devil's fiery darts will cease.

With the helmet of salvation
your head must be shod,
The sword of the Spirit,
which is the Word of God,
Here's your protection from the devil's tricks.
The Armor of God, found in Ephesians six.

Hymns

Alas, and Did My Savior Bleed
Christ the Lord is Risen Today
Faith of Our Fathers

Greek Alphabet

New Testament
MASTERY REVIEW
Cycle 12
12

1 John 4:16

God is love.

ο Θεός είναι αγάπη.

O Theós eínai agápi.

John 1:1

In the beginning was the Word,
and the Word was with God,
and God was the Word.

Ἐν ἀρχῇ ἦν ὁ λόγος,
καὶ ὁ λόγος ἦν πρὸς τὸν θεόν,
καὶ θεὸς ἦν ὁ λόγος

En ar-KAY ayn ha LOH-gohs,
ki ha LOH-gohs ayn pros ton theos.
kī theos nee LOH-gohs.

1 Corinthians 15:50-58

I declare to you, brothers and
sisters, that flesh and blood cannot
inherit the kingdom of God, nor
does the perishable inherit the
imperishable.

Listen, I tell you a mystery: We will
not all sleep, but we will all be
changed—

in a flash, in the twinkling of an eye,
at the last trumpet. For the trumpet
will sound, the dead will be raised
imperishable, and we will be
changed.

For the perishable must clothe
itself with the imperishable, and
the mortal with immortality.

When the perishable has been
clothed with the imperishable, and
the mortal with immortality, then
the saying that is written will come
true: "Death has been swallowed
up in victory."

"Where, O death, is your victory?
Where, O death, is your sting?"

The sting of death is sin, and the
power of sin is the law.

But thanks be to God! He gives us
the victory through our Lord Jesus
Christ.

Therefore, my dear brothers and
sisters, stand firm. Let nothing
move you. Always give yourselves
fully to the work of the Lord,
because you know that your labor
in the Lord is not in vain.

John 14:1-3

"Do not let your hearts be troubled.
You believe in God; believe also in
me.

My Father's house has many rooms;
if that were not so, would I have
told you that I am going there to
prepare a place for you?

And if I go and prepare a place for
you, I will come back and take you
to be with me that you also may be
where I am.

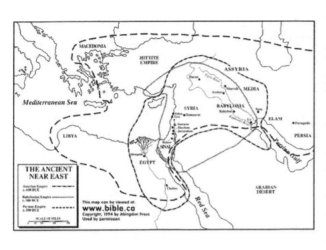

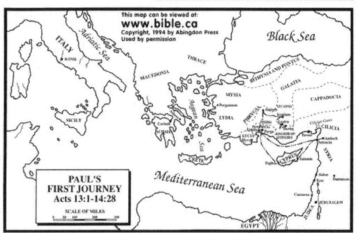

Recommended Resources

Hebrew for Christians is a superb resource for learning and practicing Hebrew. They have helpful resources like this practice grid, flashcards, and alphabet worksheets. Check out their website: hebrew4christians.com.

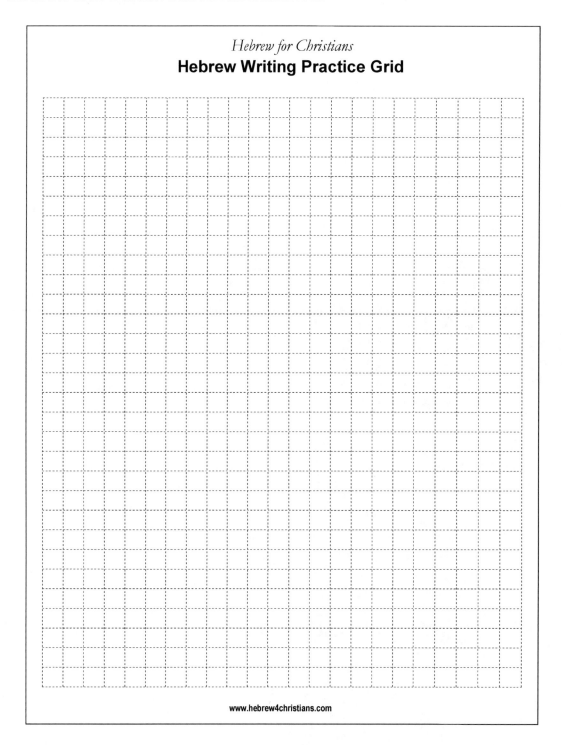

Hebrew for Christians
Hebrew Writing Practice Grid

www.hebrew4christians.com

Kidsgreek.com offers resources for young people learning New Testament Greek.

What's next?

Where do you head when your child has absorbed all this data and is ready to move on to the next phase of his Classical Education? If your child is ready to begin synthesizing what he's learned, I highly recommend The Bible Project. Their videos are the best resource I've encountered for kids (and adults) who are trying to "put all the pieces together." Look them up at thebibleproject.com.

Made in United States
Orlando, FL
12 December 2023

40693921R00100